LIVING WITH A LEGEND

LIVING WITH A
—— LEGEND ——

Kathy Botham

GRAFTON BOOKS
A Division of the Collins Publishing Group

LONDON GLASGOW
TORONTO SYDNEY AUCKLAND

Grafton Books
A Division of the Collins Publishing Group
8 Grafton Street, London W1X 3LA

Published by Grafton Books 1987

British Library Cataloguing in Publication Data
Botham, Kathy
Living with a Legend
1. Botham, Ian   2. Cricket players—
England—Biography
I. Title
796.35'8'0924   GV915.B58

ISBN 0-246-13221-3

Printed in Great Britain by
Mackays of Chatham Ltd, Kent

For Ian,
Liam, Sarah and Becky
with my love

Contents

Acknowledgements

I am lucky to have been able to rely at all times upon the support of my family, not least in the writing of this book. To my mother in particular I say 'thank you' for drawing so extensively on her memory and for her unfailing help and encouragement.

Thanks, too, to Gordon Smith, Alan Herd and Anne Kirby for giving me the incentive to start, guiding me throughout and finally crossing the 't's and dotting the 'i's.

Preface

Because so much has been written and said about Ian's and
my life together – some truth, many half-truths intermixed
with myth, and much pure fiction ('legendary' in the
proper sense of the word) – I feel that it is time now to put
the real truth into print, and to share with others, many of
whom have been our friends and supporters, the background to the happenings in our life.

For ten years of our married life I avoided the spotlight,
believing that one person in a family taking centre stage is
quite enough. I refused many interviews, avoided the press,
protected our children from the harshness of fame, and
was, for the most part, content to remain at home, a wife
and mother.

The events of March 1986 when Ian was accused of sex
orgies and drug abuse during the West Indian tour are
described in the opening chapter of this book. It was this
episode which forced me, unwillingly, under public scrutiny. Not just the British press but the international media
were focusing on me – the wronged woman, as I was
thought to be. It was then that I re-thought my life. If I
had to be in the spotlight, then so be it, but I would make
it work *for* me.

This is *my* story – all the excitement, the fun and the
confusion of living with a man some have described as a
'living legend'.

1

Trouble in Barbados

Once upon a time – isn't that how all good fairy-stories begin? The 'Miss Lindy Fields Affair' or 'The Barbados Incident' was just that – a fairy-story, but not a good one. When Ian is away from home I work on a part-time basis for my father. One Thursday in February 1986, while the England team was touring the West Indies, I was sitting in the office at the factory when my mother rang to say that she had had two telephone calls from the press asking about the possibility of interviewing me. This intrigued and puzzled me, as Ian's name had not appeared in the papers for some time, nothing of any importance had happened so far as I knew and now, within the space of two hours, two separate newspapers had rung. Warning bells sounded, unease stirred in me and the familiar niggling symptoms of worry appeared.

I couldn't concentrate on my work so I decided to ring Ian's solicitor, Alan Herd. Alan is based in London and, having his ears firmly to the ground around Fleet Street, he usually picks up the latest gossip and the so-called 'scoops' that are about to appear. On this occasion he knew nothing so, my worries somewhat assuaged, I returned to work.

Another telephone call from a third newspaper followed so I asked my mother to ring Chrissie Garbutt, a journalist

with the *Daily Mirror* and our friend, to ask if she had
heard anything. She hadn't, but we decided that she would
write a general chit-chat article about Ian and me and so
possibly divert any rumours that might be about to fly in
our direction. This seemed to be the end of it. I didn't hear
from any more newspapers and I didn't really find out
why they wanted to talk to me. It may just have been a
false alarm but, being a suspicious person, I began to
wonder what was to come. Most of the newspapers'
interest in this tour was concentrated on Graham Gooch
(whose presence in the West Indies was causing controversy because he had played in South Africa) but nevertheless I had the uneasy feeling that Ian and Kathy Botham
were waiting their turn to hit the headlines.

Ian did make the headlines, in fact, but not in the way
that we expected. 'Recluse' and 'Hermit Botham' were
some that now started to appear. It was reported that he
was staying in his room listening to tapes, eating only in
his room, entertaining in his room and in general going
out only to play cricket or to practise. The headlines and
reports became gloomier. It was implied that Botham was
'a brooding presence', that he didn't help with the younger,
less experienced players and that his current attitude was
not good for team morale.

I knew these reports to be partly true, they tallied with
the telephone calls I had received from him in which he
sounded thoroughly fed up and out of sorts. He had had
very mixed feelings about going on tour and at one time
had almost decided to withdraw. Only loyalty to his team-
mates and to England had kept him there. There were
many reasons for his reluctance to tour, but Ian is difficult
to fathom and does not always reveal his innermost
thoughts, even to me. He was returning to touring after a
break of almost two years, during which time he had
learned what family life was all about. Our new daughter,

Rebecca, was only two months old and Ian then, as now, idolized her. Only forty-eight hours before Ian flew off to the Caribbean she had been rushed into hospital for an emergency hernia operation and he hated leaving her. Also, I believe, the charity walk from John O'Groats to Land's End in aid of leukaemia had drained him mentally if not physically. We had had a very difficult Christmas following the end of the walk and it was certainly not one of the happiest periods of our marriage. Ian was finding it impossible to settle back into everyday life after the total absorption that the walk had demanded and the acclaim that it had generated. He was restless and much more demanding than usual. A few days in Hong Kong on business was a respite in what seemed to be a very troubled time. We arrived back from Hong Kong just in time for him to jet off to the West Indies.

It is significant in view of what was to follow that almost his parting words were 'Well, they won't get headlines this time because they won't see me.' He was obviously putting as much energy and effort into fading into obscurity as he did into everything else, so that even immuring himself behind a closed door to play dominoes, Trivial Pursuits and cards was beginning to generate as much interest as hitting centuries on the cricket field.

I was disturbed by the fact that he telephoned me almost every night – and not only by the cost of the calls! He seemed to want to talk to me, to the children, to any friends who were around at the time, in fact to anyone who was a link with home. One day Susie Emburey, wife of John who was also on tour and who is a very good friend of mine, telephoned, and during our conversation she slipped in the question 'Is there anything wrong with Ian?' She said that John was very worried about him because he spent such a lot of time in his room: 'None of the boys can get him to go out, not even into the bar in the hotel for a drink.'

In fact, the only time Ian sounded cheerful was during one telephone call when he reported that Allan Lamb had slightly injured his leg by jumping into a bush to avoid being photographed with a girl who had been lurking near him. When Allan had seen a camera pointing in his direction he remembered the warning that a certain Sunday newspaper was paying girls to get close enough to be photographed with the cricketers for its gossip column, so he took avoiding action as quickly as possible. Ian told me this with great glee, not, I hasten to add, because he was pleased that Allan had hurt himself but because he saw this as a vindication of his policy of cutting himself off from the possibility of this type of thing happening to him.

For several weeks my father had been undecided about going to Barbados for the fourth Test. He had almost made up his mind not to go but, in view of Ian's telephone calls, I persuaded him to change his mind, knowing that Ian would be pleased to see him and that, in the company of his father-in-law, he would surely feel safe to leave his room! I would have loved to have gone out myself but arrangements had already been made for me to fly out to Antigua for the fifth and final Test. Also, with three children, two dogs, four geese and a house to make arrangements for, it is not easy to drop everything and leave. It would have meant leaving the children for a lengthy spell and this I was and am not prepared to do. I found myself in that most difficult of positions, torn between the needs of my husband and my children.

The next few telephone calls from Ian were much happier. They were full of the fun that he and Dad and Les Taylor, Ian's room-mate, were having together, and of rescuing Dad from the rum bars where they played dominoes with the West Indian fishermen. Ian's culinary skills were also being brought into play, and I heard about the fry-ups the three of them had, with Ian as the head chef – quite often some of the other cricketers would call in for a snack, as the smell drifted around the hotel complex. Once he telephoned just before he set off for Mick Jagger's home – about a quarter of an hour's ride from Bridgetown – for dinner, together with Dad, Les Taylor, David Willis (Bob Willis's brother), Caroline (Bob's wife Juliette's sister) and Caroline's friend, Lindy Fields, an ex-Miss Barbados.

It is at times like these that I feel somewhat deflated: when I put the phone down I felt I wanted to be there to join in the fun. There have been several occasions when having a family to care for has precluded me from participating in the high spots of Ian's career, but I don't usually have long to brood on this as something invariably happens to jolt me back to the reality of motherhood.

Easter brought with it our annual family holiday in the Lake District, but for the first time in twelve years we were without Ian. Dad arrived back from Barbados, travelling straight to the Lakes, and I was able to catch up with all the latest information about how the tour was going. He told me about the very pleasant dinner party they had had at Mick Jagger's and of how Mick's girlfriend Jerry Hall had made them all welcome. They had had quite a bit of fun at Lindy Fields' expense because she had offered to come along with Caroline and David to show them the way to the house, saying that she knew it well, but then had had to stop to ask for directions, having arrived at the same crossroads for the third time. Perhaps, in retrospect, this should have been a warning that she was not all that she seemed, but at the time they treated it as a huge joke – women having no sense of direction, and all that sort of thing.

Towards the end of that Easter holiday Ian rang to ask us to look at an article in the *Sunday Mirror* in which it stated that a *Mirror* reporter, Mark Souster, had interviewed my father at his hotel in the West Indies. Dad was quoted as saying: 'Ian is on the point of giving up the game. He has never had any support from the TCCB.' Ian knew that my father would never have said any such thing. Dad was particularly annoyed as he has always had a good rapport with the other cricketers and many of the administrators of the game, and he much resented the suggestion that he would talk to members of the press other than socially.

Alan Herd is always part of the Lake District holiday, so he was able to cast a legal eye over the article. He rang the editor who at first stated that any report he printed would without doubt be true. Later, however, having spoken to Mark Souster, he had to apologize and admit that in fact Mr Souster and my father had never met but that Souster had spoken to a mutual friend and the inference was that these were Dad's thoughts. We are still not sure who the mutual friend was. To the *Sunday Mirror*'s credit they agreed to apologize the following week and sent a reporter to interview my father with a view to writing an article to set the record straight. In the event I don't think this was ever printed because it was overtaken by the events of the following weekend.

Friday 4 April saw me at my parents' home in Thorne, Yorkshire, being interviewed for *Woman* magazine by Bev Gilligan. This was an unusual occurrence for me as I had made a conscious decision years earlier to keep myself and the children out of the limelight as much as possible. Having Ian in the spotlight was as much as one family should be expected to cope with. The children were still on holiday and we decided to stay for the weekend. The photographer was able to take some family photographs and the interview went well. Afterwards we were chatting over a cup of tea and I joked, 'Possibly at this very minute someone somewhere is dreaming up another Botham fairy-tale. We've had drugs. They've had a go at his cricket, his weight, him sitting alone in his hotel bedroom. The next one's got to be another woman.' I must have been psychic.

At half-past seven that evening the phone rang. I lifted the receiver and heard a click-click-click; then came the long fuzzy pause that denotes an overseas call. Cautiously I said, 'Hello,' knowing that at that time Ian would actually be on the field of play.

A voice said, 'Hi, Kath, Crash here. How are you?' Crash, Chris Lander, is Ian's ghost-writer for his *Sun* articles.

'Hello, Crash, fine thanks. What the hell are you ringing me for? Is everything all right?'

'Yes, yes. Ian would just like to know where you're going to be in about four hours' time.'

'I'm staying here for the weekend. Why? Is he all right?'

'Er, um, er, well, yes. He just wanted me to pass this message on. Must go, he's bowling well. Someone else needs the phone. Love to everybody.'

I put the receiver down very puzzled and very apprehensive. Half an hour later the phone rang again and my mother, grandmother and I looked at each other.

Click-click-click, fuzzy pause. 'Er, hi, Kath. Crash again. Ian's just sent a note. Is there any chance of you flying out sooner – like tomorrow – with the children, of course?'

'What the hell's going on, Crash?'

'Er, um, er, well, er, nothing. Don't worry, it's all under control. Must go, Both has just taken another wicket. He's really bowling well.'

In the meantime Grandma reached for the sherry bottle and produced three glasses. We sat and speculated on what could be happening. Suddenly I decided to take action.

'I'm going to ring Alan,' I announced, 'he may know

something.' Alan answered quickly. 'I've had a couple of very peculiar phone calls from Crash, Alan. Do you know anything about what's going on?'

'Have you spoken to Ian?'

'Not yet. Apparently he's ringing me immediately play ends.'

'I think Ian ought to talk to you. Don't worry about it. There are always rumours and stories flying around about Ian. It's probably just another one of those. Don't worry. If you need me you know where I am.'

About an hour later, immediately after the tea interval, Crash, having spoken to Ian, rang again: 'Er, um, er, Kath, Crash here. Just spoken to Both, he wants you all to come over here tomorrow. He'll explain everything when he phones. Don't worry, everything is under control.'

By this time I'd had enough. My nerves had got the better of me. My suspicions were confirmed. 'Bloody hell, Crash, just what is going on? I can't talk to Ian now and I'm not prepared to wait another few hours.'

'I think it's better that Ian tells you.'

'You're obviously not going to tell me anything, Crash. Just answer yes or no to this question: is it another woman?'

'Er, um, well, er, yes, but the story is so ridiculous. You've got absolutely nothing to worry about.'

'Thought so. Thanks, Crash.' Down went the phone.

I turned to my grandma who was waiting anxiously. 'Pour the sherry out, Grandma,' I said, 'it *is* another woman.'

'Oh what a relief!' she sighed. 'Ian wouldn't do anything like that,' and we all laughed.

For the next few hours Grandma, who rarely if ever drinks, helped us to polish off a bottle of Croft's Original while we discussed every possibility – drugs, rape, sex – our stories becoming wilder as time went on.

At exactly 11.10 p.m. our time, the phone rang again. Click-click-click, long fuzzy pause. This time it was Ian.

'So it's finally happened,' I said. 'This time it's another woman. Well, we've been expecting this one.'

'Yes, you wouldn't believe the story. Do you remember me telling you we met a girl called Lindy Fields, an ex-Miss Barbados? She's claiming that we had a fling together. I'm not sure about anything else. Alan and Crash are trying to find out. We think she's tied up with Vicky Hodge. You know, the woman who claimed she'd had a passionate night of love with Prince Andrew.'

I interjected, 'Oh yes, you told me *she'd* been trying to contact you.'

'It really isn't worth worrying about, Kath. I want you and the children to come out – now.'

I told Ian that that was impossible. I had already made arrangements to travel the following Tuesday. There was no point in rearranging everything and, besides, I was determined not to give anyone the chance to say that I was flying out hot-foot to 'save' my marriage. Ian also told me that the *Sun* had offered to send one of their reporters, Hugh Whittow, to our home to fend off the rest. At the time I didn't really feel this was necessary as Andy Withers, Ian's personal assistant, was already on his way there, but Ian felt that he would be happier if I accepted their offer.

After this phone-call with Ian I no longer felt that this was going to be a major disaster.

When my father returned from the local rugby union club we filled him in on the events of the evening and he burst into laughter. 'Well,' he remarked, 'what a joke! Don't forget that I was there with Ian and nothing happened. Whatever they say there's no way at all you can believe it.'

I went to bed quite happy, but the next morning the

niggling worries returned. I rang Ian's parents to warn them and decided to go home earlier than arranged with baby Becky, leaving my two elder children, Liam and Sarah, with their grandparents who would shield them from anything likely to upset them.

Having arranged with Alan Herd that he would inform me at once if anything appeared in the *News of the World* – he would pick up one of the first copies which appear in Fleet Street about 10.30 on Saturday evening – I spent the evening packing, settling Becky into bed, rechecking arrangements and doing the thousand and one mundane things a busy housewife with three children has to do before leaving for a two-week holiday.

Andy arrived, closely followed by Hugh and a photographer. It was intended that they should write a small article to squash any story that might appear in the *News of the World*. As the drama unfolded, panic set in. Susie Emburey rang, having just returned from Barbados. She had promised Ian that she would ring us to say how much he was missing us all and to tell me how great Ian and Les Taylor, one of the other England cricketers, had been with Claire and Chloe, her two children. She also told me that the sooner I got out the better as, following my father's return, Ian was again shutting himself away in his room. He had taken some ice-cream round for Claire and Chloe and it had taken a great deal of persuasion to get him to stay for a drink with them. Knowing what was about to be 'revealed' in the press, this piece of information seemed somewhat ironic. Susie knew nothing of the rumours and when I poured out the events to her she just couldn't believe it. She told me later that she was 'stunned'; at the time she just said 'That's so unfair and untrue. How can they do it?' and replaced the receiver in tears.

Sitting in the lounge and making small-talk with two complete strangers and Andy was very difficult. Ten-thirty

came and went so I calmly got up to phone Alan Herd as
arranged. Julie, his wife, obviously under pressure as well,
told me that Alan was having difficulty in getting hold of
a copy of the paper and would ring me as soon as he'd
managed to get one. The minutes seemed endless. My heart
was thumping and I felt sick; not knowing meant that I
was unable to take control of the situation. The fairy-story
was beginning to resemble a nightmare.

Near midnight the phone rang. I was very tempted to
let it ring but knew I couldn't. Hugh told me later I had
appeared to be very cool, calm and collected.

'Kath?'

'Hello, Alan.'

'Kath. Is anybody there with you?'

'Yes, Andy and the chappies from the *Sun*, but they're
in the lounge.'

'Kath, you've got to know. It's not pleasant, it's awful.
It's worse than anything that has been printed before.
There are five pages and it's very explicit.'

'What do you mean, "explicit"? Is it drugs, sex or what?'

'It's everything!'

I told him that I didn't want to know any more. I was
perfectly all right. Would he please ring my parents. Alan
told me that I should say nothing to the *Sun* reporters at
that time and asked to speak to them. They were extremely
understanding and left saying how sorry they were and
that if I needed anything at all they would be there.

Andy poured me a large gin and tonic and for a while
we sat in stunned silence. All of a sudden I hurled one of
my best cut-glasses across the room. Gin and tonic went
everywhere but the glass didn't break! Then I fled into
Becky's room and sat on the bed, staring at my baby. I
had never felt so alone.

The telephone broke into my thoughts. It was Ian. At
first he sounded quite cheerful, but at this stage I was

trembling with fear, and possibly hatred, of this man who, however unwittingly, had brought this upon me. I became hysterical. Ian tried to calm me down and eventually he too broke down in tears of anger and frustration and sadness and handed the phone to Crash. Crash also didn't know what to say and could only repeat that I mustn't believe it, that Ian loved us all greatly and would never do anything to jeopardize our life together. I don't remember if I went to bed that night but I do remember that I was dreading Sunday morning.

In fact, Sunday brought very little news. My friends from the *Sun* returned in the early morning for my protection, but I had not bargained on the fact that most of the press didn't know my new address or telephone number. However, my parents and Ian's parents were inundated with telephone calls and press arrivals. My parents' next-door neighbour and good friend Dolores Wilson called in to see if she could help in any way, having seen the constant stream of unwelcome visitors. She took Liam and Sarah off and out of the way for the day, as by now they too had realized that something pretty serious was going on. Dolores told us later that Liam was beside himself with rage at the press intrusion; we had used Thorne as a retreat, so for the media to find us there was, I think, the last straw for him.

For years we had fended off reporters with 'No comment', 'We have nothing to say' – but this time we were adamant that we would say something. Ian's parents, Les and Marie, rang my parents. They are good friends and get on very well together. While they were discussing the situation yet another reporter arrived and overheard my mother saying, 'It's yet another Botham fairy-tale.' He liked that and asked if he could use it for a headline. I think he was quite surprised that, for once, he was invited in and treated to a few well-chosen words.

In fact, most of Monday's press were quite supportive. They had done some research into Miss Lindy Fields and come up with a few unsavoury facts about her. I often wonder about the BBC news; in their coverage on Sunday they actually showed the *News of the World* front page and made sure that those millions who don't actually purchase the newspaper knew what had been printed. Is this really what the BBC think of as newsworthy? I found it highly questionable for the BBC, which has such a reputation for respectability, to use the *News of the World* as a basis for their news item.

As for the ex-Miss Barbados, Lindy Fields, I later did a little research of my own and came up with some interesting information which perhaps I had better keep to myself at this stage as I don't want to be accused of stirring this up all over again or being unnecessarily bitter. Sufficient to say I know what I know.

It might be appropriate to mention at this point that, on the team's arrival in Barbados, Ian had received a telephone call at his hotel, and I quote: 'Ian? Vicky Hodge here. We haven't met but I know you must get tired of all the hassle. If you want a quiet drink and relaxation do come and visit me. I have a villa out here which will give you some privacy.' Ian replaced the receiver and joked to my father who was with him at the time, 'Vicky Hodge! I need her like I need a hole in the head,' and promptly forgot about her.

Unfortunately he was not able to dismiss Lindy quite so easily.

Juliette Willis and her sister Caroline went to Barbados to join Bob and his brother David. On their arrival contact was made between Caroline and Lindy who had been quite good friends during Lindy's spell in England with her husband. David was taken by Caroline to meet Miss Fields for lunch. David's assessment of Lindy is interesting: 'She was an obvious extrovert, loud, excitable, brassy and a name-dropper. We hadn't been in her company long before she was telling us of the famous names she had been to bed with.' David also remembers her saying: 'These cricketers, they're really wonderful. I'd love to meet Ian Botham, he's a bit of a star.'

She was then taken by Caroline to the hotel complex where the team was staying and introduced into the cricketing scene. On tours many relatives and friends of the players arrive and all are taken at face value so, although she was not everyone's cup of tea, Lindy was made welcome and was invited along to Test matches by the Willis clan. She was 'in' – and what good use she made of the opportunity!'

As the events of that dreadful weekend unfolded hour by hour and I began to piece together bits of the story, I looked at some of the photographs of her which appeared in Monday's papers. I felt absolutely nothing. I suppose that the mind produces its own kind of anaesthesia. I went through the procedures of saying goodbye to our children, secure in the knowledge that they would be well looked after by nanny Diane and supported by the headmaster and staff of their school.

Monday evening I arrived back at Thorne to spend the evening with my parents. This would enable us to have an early start to Heathrow the next morning. As I turned into St Nicholas Road, the street where I lived as a child, and where my parents still live, I was astonished by the traffic. Cars and television cameras all over the place and strangers mingled with a few familiar faces. I really couldn't believe the furore that had been caused and genuinely couldn't understand the interest in me.

That evening and the next morning the postman, milk-man and several callers found themselves the subject of media interest. Schoolchildren going to school at the end of the road found it very absorbing and, in the end, our neighbours called the police to move the cameras along both for our sakes and their own as they found it difficult to move to and from their houses.

I flew to Antigua on Tuesday evening with Chrissie Garbutt and Hugh Whittow, who were an enormous help. Francis de Souza, who works for British Airways, helped us to clear flight procedures and put us into the club-class lounge before anyone really knew we were there. Our seats, originally booked under the names of Botham and Garbutt, were left vacant as we had been upgraded into club class and we were now flying as Kathy Smith and Christine Jones – alias Smith and Jones. Passenger lists were brought along and I was warned of the press who had been booked on to the flight. I remember a *Daily Mail* photographer called Monty Fresco looking at me every time I moved. He was just as you see in films, trying to pretend he wasn't there, holding a newspaper up to his face and peering over the top of it.

I seemed to float through the next few hours still in a state of shock. Everyone was very kind but I remember becoming more and more nervous about meeting Ian.

The numbing effect of the shock began to wear off as we landed at Antigua. It is a very tiny airport and I could see rows of cameras from the plane windows. I walked down the steps feeling I must smile, so I did, pinning a look of fixed happiness to my face. I was put into an electric buggy and whizzed off to meet Ian privately. I was so dazed I didn't see him at first, though he was standing right in front of me. The cameramen were in ecstasy as we gave each other a perfunctory kiss and the sky lit up with flash-bulbs. Questions were hurled at us but we really had nothing to say. We were both absolutely amazed at the way this insignificant story had pushed us on to the front pages. I say 'insignificant story' now, but at the time,

although I was sure that it *was* just that, I wanted to hear
Ian himself tell me so.

We were both nervous and didn't know what to say. All
I could do was nod and twist my hands nervously as Ian
tried to engage me in what was very strained conversation.
Viv Richards also came to the airport. He greeted us and
then went out to involve the press in conversation while
we slipped away through the back.

We drove to the hotel in silence but as soon as our room
door closed behind us I found my voice. I had to raise the
subject of the Lindy Fields 'incident' with Ian when at last
we were on our own. Our conversation on the matter
lasted all of five seconds. Neither Ian nor I are without
fault but the one thing we don't do is lie to each other.
Living apart as much as we do, we have to trust each other.

If this was a fairy-story, at this point I would have
melted into Ian's arms, soft lights would have magically
appeared and a full-scale orchestra would have struck up
discreetly in the background. We would have declared our
undying love for each other and been ready to face the
world together and if necessary alone in a sea of accusa-
tions and mistrust, treating hostility and suspicion with
contempt, happy just to be together.

In reality it doesn't work like that – at least not for me.
Yes, I believed Ian, I still do, but the pain and degradation
of being headlined by the world's press in such a way was
always with me. To some women, perhaps to Lindy Fields
for example, this obviously wouldn't matter; they thrive
on such publicity. To me such publicity is anathema; my
children, at the ages of six and eight, had to face their
schoolfriends and were very vulnerable to taunts in the
school playground; Ian's parents and my parents had to
face friends and neighbours and the probings of the ever-
attentive media; our good friends and close relations who
so ably supported us were all touched by what happened

and what was said about us. All these people swam in and out of my thoughts. Our future life together and what it was likely to hold (I didn't really think about the enormity of the present) was my main concern.

It was a very difficult two weeks. People were extremely kind. Some people would not talk about the matter to me, although I wanted to talk about it. I usually shrank from television, but found that the 'Breakfast Time' interview we did with Frank Bough was quite a relief because I could talk about it at last. The one person people *did* talk about was Lindy Fields, and no one had a good word to say about her.

Gradually our holiday took on the semblance of normality. The final Test match had started so Ian was occupied during the day. I didn't go to watch much – I never do – but spent my days sunbathing and chatting with friends, trying to relax, gradually pulling myself out of the fits of depression I was apt to fall into.

People I hardly knew tried to help us in many ways. One lady took me to see a holiday villa she had offered us for a week or two following the Test match. 'You need time together,' she said. 'Do come and see it, you'll love it.' It was a lovely place and on our return we stopped off at her home to have a cup of tea. I arrived back at the hotel much later than I had intended and, as I hadn't expected to be late, I hadn't left a message for Ian. He was beside himself with worry. My mood of the previous days had upset him and I really think he wondered whether I had taken myself off home or worse. He had searched and rung everywhere he could think of, trying to locate me. I was greeted on my return in the hotel lobby by Chrissie: 'Where on earth have you been? Ian's beside himself with worry. He's been looking for you everywhere.'

The pleasant day had lifted my spirits and I dashed up to our room. We had decided to eat in our room that evening, so I set a table and bought a bottle of Ian's favourite wine. Bob Willis offered to bring in a large pizza for us later on.

Ian returned and was relieved to find me in such good spirits. He hadn't had a very good day cricket-wise. He was close to the bowling record for Test match wickets and had hoped that this match might clinch it, but it hadn't – so, for a change, I set about cheering him up. He suggested that we should go down to the hotel bar and have a drink with anyone who might be there, which I was pleased to do.

We found several of the cricketers there and had a good laugh and chat. Ian was taken into a corner by Simon, a friend of Allan Lamb and his wife Lindsay, who had some information for him about Lindy Fields.

Ian came dashing over to tell me this information. I suppose he felt that he had found a nail for the coffin in which he could bury this story and hoped that the news would make me feel good. In fact it had the opposite effect. I didn't want to hear Lindy Fields' name spoken again. I began to cry. Ian looked at me in amazement and said, 'For God's sake, what's the matter with you? Cheer up.' I got up and fled to my room. We had got over the worst, the way ahead was clearing now and I was crying as if my heart was breaking and I didn't really know why.

Ian followed me upstairs and spoke calmly to me. Bob appeared with the pizza – jumbo size – and we chatted to him as if nothing was wrong. He left and we settled down to eat. I was feeling sorry for myself and was morose and sullen. Suddenly Ian went berserk. He jumped out of his chair, grabbed the pizza and flung it across the room. Cheese, tomato, bits of this and that went everywhere. He rampaged around the room picking things up and hurling them down. Clothes, shoes, make-up went winging around. I fled to the bed and crouched there. The bedclothes were pulled off and flung to the floor, sending the bedside-lamp flying. The wine bucket filled with ice hurtled through the air. In ten years of marriage I had never seen Ian like this and I was terrified, but he didn't touch me. Eventually his rage abated and he rushed out of the room and disappeared from the hotel. I was left to survey the damage.

I rang Bob who came immediately. He stood in shocked silence, genuinely upset for both of us. Then he wondered aloud how much more either of us could take. We contacted Chrissie and another friend, Colleen Rumsey, and between us we cleaned up the room. The only casualty was the bedside lamp for which we apologized and paid for a replacement.

We were all frantically worried about Ian: no one had seen him and the area was bristling with reporters eager for a good story about us. Bob went looking for him with no success, but eventually Ian returned very much the worse for wear and feeling terribly sorry for himself. 'Our marriage is finished,' he said. 'We've been trapped by the headlines.' He blamed me for everything, telling me I had no faith in him and that it was quite obvious we could no longer live together. Then he collapsed on to the remade bed and fell into a deep sleep.

I lay awake convinced that what he had said was true. I didn't think I could take any more long separations, bringing up the children virtually on my own, as well as the media attention and all that went with it. During that long night I convinced myself that we would all be better off apart and rehearsed how I should tell the children. We had tried so hard but outside forces had beaten us.

In the early hours of the morning I must have drifted into an uneasy sleep for I woke to the full light of day with Ian still stretched out like a log beside me. I glanced around the room and my gaze stopped at the curtain tracking.

There, festooning down from the track was a piece of
pizza with melted cheese hanging like a yellow icicle from
it. I broke into laughter which woke Ian. His gaze followed
my pointing finger and he too laughed. He lifted me up
and I extricated it, thankful to see that it had left no mark.

The events of the previous evening were never mentioned again. Although I sulked a little during that day,
Ian was very tolerant. It was the rest day in the Test match
and we went out on a boat for the day with friends and
gradually I began to enjoy myself once more. Nowadays
when Ian shows any sign of annoyance I just look at him
and say, 'Are there any flying pizzas around?'

I believe our marriage is now stronger than ever, and the
one thing that this period of time gave me was a determination to make the spotlight work for me. If I had to live
in the glare of publicity then I would make the most of it
and not hide myself away as I had done hitherto.

2

Life before Botham

I suppose it was inevitable that at some time during my life I should become involved in the cricketing scene. My mother tells me that one of her earliest memories is of turning over in bed in the early hours of the morning trying to shut out the sound of crackles and whistles while her cricket-mad father in the room below listened to the pre-satellite commentary on the fortunes of our Test team down under. The same cricket-mad grandfather, on hearing of my safe arrival and having secretly wished for a boy, said, 'Oh, lovely, a little girl! Well, Gerry, she'll just have to play tennis for England instead of cricket.' Sadly, he didn't live to meet Ian.

My childhood was happy and fairly uneventful, which is really just as well; I feel as though I spent the first nineteen years of my life on a more-or-less even keel, charging up my batteries for what was to come later!

Being born in Doncaster of Yorkshire parents is a basic qualification, I am led to believe, for writing a book which is concerned with cricket. I have lived most of my life in Yorkshire and I am sure there is no place quite like it. A fact that Ian does not dispute, although at times his assessment is less than complimentary.

My parents and grandparents have lived in Thorne for many years. They seem to know almost everyone, in turn everyone knows them. My sister, Lindsay, and I enjoyed living there very much, mostly because we always felt that we belonged.

As with most people, my early 'memories' are a mixture of what I really remember and those incidents which become part of family history and are handed down in 'do you remember?' sessions.

My maternal grandfather was the postmaster of Thorne and as such would see many people during a day's work. His customers would go into the office and tell him that they had seen us, and on the frequent visits he made to us he would reel off our movements for that day. Lindsay and I were always amazed that he knew so much about us and really believed that he owned 'the magic television' he used to tell us about.

My grandmother was an endless source of dolls' clothes and books, and Lindsay and I looked forward to Mondays when she would come for the evening. We were allowed to stay up later than usual, first to watch 'Coronation Street' then Harry Worth. Grandma would later bath and put us to bed – always ready to read us our favourite stories.

When we were both at school my mother returned to teaching. She was unable to get home for lunch so, as our infant school was almost next door to our other grandparents' house, Grandma and Grandpa Waller had the pleasure of giving us lunch. It was a pleasure for all of us, I am sure. They had three sons and five grandsons and we were the only girls. Grandma gave free rein to her hitherto thwarted desires to make little girls' clothes and buy little girls' toys. She had been one of eight children. Her father, a village schoolmaster from Broughton, Lincolnshire, had demanded of his children a high standard of obedience and thrift, giving love and care in return. This she instilled into us, teaching us to knit, sew and mend.

At this time my father was working away from home as works manager for the Premier Drum Company in Leicester. He came home once midweek and at weekends. These were always busy times when we visited friends, had visitors in return, gardened and played and worked. We were spoiled, I think, to the extent that all little girls have a right to be. There were limits, though, and we generally knew how far to go. One of the limits was untidiness. Mum would let things go so far then, usually following a bad day's teaching, we would arrive home to find the hall knee-deep in coats, bags, scarves, books, shoes, records, etcetera, and a stony-faced mother demanding that they should be put immediately in their rightful places. As seventy-five per cent of this was invariably Lindsay's (no doubt she will dispute this) at the time I couldn't understand why I was still putting things away in drawers and cupboards long after she had finished and was downstairs reading or playing the piano. It was only later that I learned her very simple method of tidying away: everything went under the bed or was stuffed into the bottom of the wardrobe.

My father then began working in London and was not able to get home so frequently. This meant, apart from our company, Mum spent a lot of time on her own. All her friends had 'nine-to-five' husbands and she felt the need to go out and make a life of her own. In a very short space of time she became a town councillor, a member of the parochial church council and sat on so many committees that we almost had to make an appointment to see her. This went on for two or three years and, looking back, I realize that we must have objected strongly and frequently because suddenly it all stopped – to our great relief.

I too find I have to spend time away from the children and when they say to me, 'You're not going away *again*, are you?' and I see the look of disappointment on their faces, I think back and know exactly how they feel. Yet knowing this doesn't prevent me from pursuing, in part, a life of my own.

On Saturday nights our parents went out and we shared a babysitter with our two friends from next door, Ronald and Jane Whitlam, taking turns to sleep in each other's houses. On these occasions we would make up plays together, one of our favourites being Peter Pan and Wendy. Ronald was Peter Pan, though as a well-respected solicitor in Sheffield I guess he won't really like me revealing this to his many clients. Lindsay was Wendy. Jane was Mrs Darling and I was Captain Hook and, occasionally, Tinker-Bell. My father took to calling me 'Tink' which stuck. I didn't mind really, except that he would do it on occasions when I wanted to be dignified – like my first grown-up party and my first visit to Lord's as Ian's wife.

Although we had no brothers we had boy cousins Timothy, Christopher and Richard, with whom we spent many happy times both in Thorne and in Somerset where they lived. We would often go into Yeovil so the chances are that Ian and I may have passed each other in the street without knowing.

A great deal of our early life was spent acting. The boys and Lindsay were very keen. I was less so but was press-ganged into taking part. We used to raise money for a children's society staging our plays in a large comfortable playhouse we christened Rose Cottage at the bottom of our garden. Our long-suffering parents and grandparents would be hauled in to watch, paying to enter, paying for orange squash and biscuits which they provided, giving generously to a collection and buying tickets for a raffle prize which they had also contributed. Recently, for my grandfather's one hundredth birthday party we again pro-duced a play and this time we had extra characters – our own husbands, wives and children who loved carrying on the tradition.

About the time I was ten, two important events happened in my life. The first was to be given my own bedroom. I have always been neat and tidy, and was irritated by my less than tidy younger sister who was always surrounded by books. I beavered about making my room just as I wanted it and it was frequently held up as an example to Lindsay. At this age I think I must have been rather insufferable. I confess to having been bossy and intolerant of many things which didn't really matter. Now I have more important things to worry about and let the minor details take care of themselves.

The second important event was that a friend of my father's got married and brought his new wife to meet us. Brian and Vivienne Close entered my life, and perhaps that was the beginning of it all.

Vivienne was well named. She was everything I wanted to be: vivacious, pretty, fun to be with. And she loved us. My parents and Brian and Viv became firm friends and we saw a great deal of them. 'Uncle' Brian was then captain of Yorkshire Cricket Club and much of my early teens was spent at Headingley or Bradford watching Yorkshire win. Mum and Dad watched too: Lindsay was there in body but spent most of her time reading.

At about this time, too, I passed the Eleven Plus and went to Thorne Grammar School. There it became clear that I was quite good at sport. I quickly established myself in the hockey team, reaching the dizzy heights of the first team in my fourth year. Tennis also became a passion of mine and I soon made the tennis teams as well. I wasn't too bad at my lessons either, but I had to work hard to achieve the results I wanted. I have always suffered from bouts of over-conscientiousness and my mother used to say to me, 'Kathryn, for goodness' sake put your books away and come downstairs for a coffee.' It's not something I have to say to my son. It takes an operation to separate him from his rugby, soccer or cricket ball. (I wonder who he takes after?)

By this time my father had given up playing Rugby Union and had taken up refereeing. He would take me along to the games and many a time I have ended up running the line as a touch judge. I became pretty wised-up about rugby and this stood me in good stead not only when I was a student and became a popular non-playing member of the Rugby Club, but also later with Liam who loves the game.

Some of the teachers at our school had earlier taught my mother and father. My Grandfather Hind was chairman of the governors so it was just as well that I was fairly well behaved as I wouldn't have got away with much. However, I was hauled before the senior mistress on several occasions for wearing my gymslip too short or, shame upon shame, painting my fingernails! She would invariably finish her lecture with the words, 'You of all people should know better', which I bitterly resented. Talking later to Lindsay we both recalled wishing that we had been able to make our own way within the school. We missed out on some things, we believe, either because certain members of the staff resented us or because they didn't wish to be making favourites of us.

On Sundays we watched cricket. In those days there was no Sunday League but Brian played for a team called Rothman's Cavaliers. One Sunday they were playing at Middlesbrough and the whole family went along to watch. We had lunch on arrival and I found myself sitting opposite Geoff Boycott and his friend Anne Wyatt. They were very friendly and very kind to Lindsay and myself. Ian and I have always got on well with Geoff and Anne and we have spent many happy times together on tours.

I'm afraid I can't say the same about Denis Compton, though. He was also at this match and I blotted my copybook when I said, 'My grandma used to like you very much when you played cricket.' As he was playing in this match I made myself distinctly unpopular. Perhaps that is why he is always so vindictive to Ian in his newspaper column. I used to think it was jealousy of someone who had usurped his crown, but perhaps it is me he is carrying a grudge against!

There is a difference in age of two and a half years between Lindsay and myself. As young children we got on extremely well, occasionally falling out but always ready to stand firmly together when the chips were down. This unanimity ceased abruptly the first time she turned round and said, 'Oh, do it yourself!' I could hardly believe it. Where had my compliant, obliging little sister gone? For the next year or so war was declared. She was extremely clever at finding just the right thing to annoy me – the principal thing being that she was extremely clever, full stop. She had excellent school results with little or no effort while I worked for hours to achieve less. She would deliberately engage my boyfriends in long conversations to delay our going out and frequently found ways and means to accompany us. Whenever I see the advertisement of the small boy being offered a chocolate cream egg as a bribe to go away by big sister's boyfriend, I think of Lindsay.

We spent many weekends and holidays with Brian and Viv Close. Their children, Lynn and Lance, were babies and I was happy to babysit and later take care of them for weekends or longer when Viv needed to be with Brian. It was then that I began to see the other side of being and living with a celebrity. I loved and admired Brian but it was clear how difficult he was to live with. I can now see many of the traits in Ian that I saw then in Brian: the selfish single-mindedness which is so difficult to incorporate into a family situation; the inability to see through people; and the great generosity, not just in financial terms but in the depth of affection they both show towards the people they like.

As I grew older and more mature in my outlook I also realized how difficult it was having a father who worked away from home and returned only for short periods of time. It was fine while our social life was contained within the family but when we began to spread our wings Dad's face often clouded in disappointment as our plans interfered with his plans for us as a family.

County cricket matches were now out. I had my own commitments both to sport and to other social gatherings, and having observed the 'groupies' hanging around hoping for a look, a kind word or even more from the cricketers, I was determined that no one should think I was becoming one of them. One or two of the younger Yorkshire players had cast a glance in my direction but I had other fish to fry nearer home. In any event it was about this time, 1971, that Brian was sacked by Yorkshire and went to Somerset. I can remember being extremely upset by this. I suppose it was the first of many cricketing upsets that would later colour my life.

The only cricket that touched my life for the next year or two was during our annual family holiday with my uncle and aunt in Somerset when we went to the Weston-super-Mare Cricket Festival to see Brian and Viv. And there was one weekend in London which I shall always remember.

For some time Brian and Viv had promised me a weekend in London as a thank-you for spending so much time with their children. Somerset, of whom Brian was now captain, had a fixture at Lord's and I was invited. In the evenings we went to the theatre and interesting restaurants, returning to join the team for drinks at the hotel. During these few days my 'O'-level results were expected and I am sure the spectators at Lord's must have wondered what on earth Brian was doing as he periodically turned round from his fielding position to peer at the stand with a questioning glance. When the expected phone call did arrive I held up eight fingers to show the number of passes and he awarded me with a silent clap. During this match Peter ('Dasher') Denning, a young Somerset cricketer, came to talk to me. He told me about his fiancée Annie, with whom I was later to become very friendly.

Incidentally, it was at the Weston-super-Mare Cricket Festival that Ian first saw me, although I don't remember seeing him. He must have been attracted towards me from the very beginning because he was able to tell me exactly what I was wearing – a pair of navy-blue hot-pants and a rather violently multi-coloured striped polo-neck sweater, long white boots and pony-tail! Ian commented to Dasher Denning at the time, 'She's a bit of all right although a bit young, and it's a horrible hair-style.' We must both have been all of sixteen.

Back at school, life became less pleasant, for a decision had to be made about my future. I really had no idea what I wanted to do but my parents were emphatic that I had to have qualifications for a career. By this time my father had started a successful small business of his own, making percussion instruments, particularly drum-sticks. We discussed all the usual professions, but I wanted none of these. 'Couldn't I just work for you?' I asked my father. 'Only if you become qualified at something first,' was his reply.

I decided on business studies with French and began sixth-form study of economics with French, German and general studies. I enjoyed my sixth form at school, contin-

uing with sport and finding a rapport with my teachers not
possible in the lower school. I still see many of them
around and enjoy stopping for a chat and a shaking of
heads over the difference between schooling then and now.

For my seventeenth birthday I had received a course of
driving lessons. Ronald, my friend from next door, offered
to accompany me as the qualified driver for a practice
drive. I had already driven up and down the long drive to
our house and on a derelict air-field, so I felt quite
confident as I collected my provisional driving licence and
set off. Half an hour later I rushed, distraught, into the
house to fetch Dad while Ronald sat in the car which was
now perched precariously over the cement kerbing stones
which lined the drive. The bonnet was pushed through the
privet hedge and the body of the car slewed at right angles,
completely blocking the drive. I had turned the corner of
the road and had just gone on cornering. To add to my
humiliation, friends and neighbours gathered to debate the
best way of removing it!

As a child I had visited many European countries, but
for my eighteenth birthday my parents arranged a trip to
Canada for me. My godmother, Heather, a very good
friend of my mother's, lives in Vancouver with her husband and sons, and I went to stay with them for a month.
They were excellent hosts and showed me much of British
Columbia. We did a lot of walking, swimming and climb-
ing among some very beautiful scenery. I'm sure they will
forgive me if I say that there was one shortish period of
time I really did not enjoy very much – camping. I had
been put off that particular hobby during my days as a girl
guide when my guide troop spent a week in continuous
torrential rain. On this occasion the weather was beautiful,
but at the age of eighteen I had grown accustomed to all
mod cons and I found it extremely difficult to be parted
from my red vanity case which contained essential items

like electric hair-curlers and make-up. Don, Heather's husband, did not believe in taking anything that was not absolutely essential, but he was extremely patient with me as I struggled to accustom myself to life in the rough, and was genuinely delighted when I made huckleberry jam from berries I had picked myself, in a can over a candle!

During my stay in Canada I learned that my 'A'-level results enabled me to take up a place at Lanchester Polytechnic. I had had a hard time persuading my head-master that I had no wish to take a university degree. As I said earlier, I found school work difficult and knew that the more practical polytechnic course would suit me better.

Back in England I embarked on a four-year business studies course. I remember my tutor saying, 'Kathryn, this list of 120 books – we are only suggesting that you dip into a few of them, you are not expected to read every one from cover to cover'!

I did not like college life at all. There were good times of course, and I made some good friends but I was glad when my first year ended and I could spent the next six months at home working for my father on the practical side of the course. During that summer at home my social life blossomed. I still had many good friends from school and I now knew more people from different parts of the country. Ronald was studying law at Cambridge and he invited me to the Cambridge May Ball; a friend from college invited me to spend a day or two at the Henley Regatta. There was also the day when my mother had to entertain one of my boyfriends in the dining room, and Lindsay, at fifteen, did a very good job of entertaining another one in the lounge while I was in the hall talking to a third on the telephone.

It was a good summer. In addition to doing marketing and secretarial work which I enjoyed, my father bought me a small car and I travelled England promoting a new range of drum-sticks he had brought out. The music industry is a small one, and through my work I met some very interesting people: Carl Palmer of Emerson, Lake and Palmer, John Bonham of Led Zeppelin, and Phil Collins of Genesis, to name a few.

On 26 June 1974 Somerset were playing a Benson and Hedges' one-day match at Grace Road, Leicester, and Brian Close had invited the family to the cricket and for a drink later that evening. Lindsay was in the middle of her 'O'-levels and as she had no exam on that day, she and Dad set off in the bright sunshine of the early afternoon. I picked Mum up from her school, having arranged to meet them at Leicester cricket ground in the early evening. I didn't really want to go; I had been away working and was expecting a boyfriend for the weekend, but I hadn't been to a cricket match for ages and I was looking forward to seeing Brian and Viv again. As we neared Leicester the heavens opened. We parked the car outside the ground and walked in. No play, sodden wicket. We headed straight for the bar to meet the others. I remember chatting to Ray Illingworth on the way there. Funny, we don't even acknowledge each other now. In fact, there are many things I remember about that day.

— 3 —

Teenage Love

The clubhouse was crowded and buzzing with noise. Lindsay and I were fed up: it isn't an atmosphere I relish at the best of times – smoke-filled bars packed with cricket supporters analysing each stroke and each ball, and all so knowledgeable. How can they all be right?

For once Brian was out from the dressing-room fairly quickly and I was relieved to see him, hopeful that we would now get away and enjoy a pleasant evening together. I should have known better. There are always so many people to talk to and have a drink with at the end of sporting occasions, cricket being no exception. Gradually one or two of the other players whom Lindsay and myself had met previously drifted in, and we were soon catching up on their news. The numbers round the table increased and I did notice one or two unfamiliar faces join us. During a lull in the conversation I turned to a young man sitting on my left and asked him if he had seen any of the cricket before it began to rain. He was somewhat taken aback and replied curtly, 'Actually, I've been playing!'

Feeling rather embarrassed, both for myself and for him, I apologized, explaining that I hadn't seen any cricket for some time. He laughed and introduced himself. The name was familiar – Ian Botham – yes, I had read it in newspaper reports about Somerset. He had recently, almost single-

handed, won a one-day match for Somerset against Hamp-
shire, having been hit in the mouth by the West Indian fast
bowler Andy Roberts with practically the first ball he
received from him.

Ian's particular friend at that time was his Somerset
team-mate Denis Breakwell, with whom he shared a flat in
Taunton, and it seemed natural that, as we already knew
Denis, Lindsay, Denis, Ian and myself should go out for a
meal together.

As we walked towards the main gates to the car, several
autograph-hunters ran up to Denis with books out-
stretched. No one asked Ian and he stood to one side
chatting to us while Denis obliged. It had started to drizzle
again. When we reached the main gates Ian inquired
pleasantly, 'Which way?' 'Left,' I replied confidently, 'it's
just down here.' As we reached the end of the road panic
set in – no car. 'It must be round the corner,' I announced.
Lindsay and Denis cast a glance at each other.

Reaching the next corner in the now pouring rain, Denis
and Lindsay disappeared into a nearby pub. 'You're sure
you do have a car here?' asked Ian.

'Of course I have. It's here somewhere.' By now we had
walked round two and a half sides of Grace Road cricket
ground. Ian grabbed my hand and we ran the other one
and a half sides to find a lonely car parked in the rain just
to the right of the main gate. We both burst out laughing
and fell into it, sopping wet. I maintain to this day that I
left it where I had said. Perhaps the fates moved it? Though
Ian asserts that I did it deliberately to gain his interest and
he often tells people now that he married me to protect me
from myself!

Having picked up Lindsay and Denis we went to a
Chinese restaurant and laughed and joked throughout the
meal – most of the jokes being told by Lindsay at my
expense. Obviously this didn't put Ian off as he wanted to

make arrangements to see me again. Somerset were playing at Derby the following weekend, but I had to tell Ian I couldn't make it because I had a friend coming. Ian's reply was, 'I hope he's nice.' We arranged that he would ring me some time.

During the next day or two I wondered whether Ian would bother to ring. From this first meeting I found him interesting and I wanted to see him again. He rang mid-week and tried to persuade me to go to Derby, but my arrangements had been made and I wouldn't alter them however much I wanted to.

Perhaps it would have been better if I had. I was poor company that weekend, and when Mum and Dad set off to go to the cricket at Derby on the Saturday I was really aggrieved. Afterwards my mother told me how very pleasant Ian had been after the match, joining them for a drink and inquiring after my health.

My Uncle Rex was deputy headmaster at Sexey's School at Bruton in Somerset and each July we were invited to the school-leavers' dinner-dance. This year I was able to make arrangements to see Ian at Taunton on the Saturday after the dance. When the day came I was strangely reluctant to go; perhaps because I was used to boyfriends coming to see me, or perhaps because this could have been construed as me chasing him.

In the event I went along to the match and duly waited for him in the clubhouse at Taunton afterwards. Unknown to me his family were also in the clubhouse and when Ian arrived, not noticing me, he immediately joined a group of people and began talking to a girl who was with them. Having been reticent about going in the first place I felt awkward and annoyed. 'Let's go,' I said to my mother, 'Ian's got a girlfriend here.' As I said it Ian caught sight of me and hurried across. 'Hi,' he said, 'come and meet Dad and my sister Dale.'

I persuaded my parents to take me to the John Player League match the following day and even managed to get them to stay on to go out for a meal with Ian and Brian after that match, which meant a very late trek back to Yorkshire. It was a meal that Brian perhaps wished we hadn't arranged as he was 'on a pair'. Having chosen duck to eat he joked that he hoped it wasn't an omen. Sure enough he got a duck the next day to complete 'the pair' (two noughts in a match) – the first time ever in his cricketing career.

I remember that meal for something else, though: my mother remarked about Ian, 'What a nice, quiet young man.' In view of Ian's somewhat exuberant personality it is odd that many people make the same comment after meeting him for the first time.

The cricket season continued with Ian travelling throughout the country managing to retain his place in the first team. He had come into the team as a replacement for the injured Tom Cartwright but having got there he was determined to do well enough to stay.

Most evenings he rang me and I frequently received flowers. He wasn't earning much and he told me later that he lived very frugally while most of his expenses went on telephone calls and flowers. As often as possible I went to watch him play and my somewhat beaten-up Austin 1100 could be seen flying across the length and breadth of England.

One morning I set off very early to travel to Canterbury where Somerset were playing Kent in a Gillette Cup match. I had persuaded Dad that the Kent area of England had lots of music shops where I was sure I could do plenty of business. This way I felt I could legitimately ask him for the day off to watch cricket and travel on expenses as well.

I arrived at Canterbury to find that there was no ticket

left for me at the gate. Ian had left it with his mother, instructing her to look out for me. As I was late and she hadn't yet met me, things had gone a little wrong. I was able to talk myself into the ground, which was full, and parked the car. I had taken clothes to change into and as the carpark appeared to be deserted I decided to change there. I wriggled out of my jeans while sitting behind the steering wheel. Just then, the friendly carpark attendant strolled up for a few words. I hastily pulled a jacket across my knees and sat there in my blouse and knickers chatting away. After what seemed hours he moved away and I was able to complete my change and dash into the ground to sit, as arranged, as near as possible to the dressing-room where I found Marie, Ian's mother.

We introduced ourselves and I realized immediately I had found a friend. We were soon chattering away nineteen to the dozen as if we had known each other for years. It was from Marie I learned that both she and Les, Ian's father, were Yorkshire-born, Bradford and Beverly respectively. She told me about Ian's two sisters, Dale and Wendy, and of nine-year-old Graeme. None of them was with her that day as it was a mid-week match and work and school took priority. I sensed that they were a close-knit family, as was my own, and I enjoyed hearing about them and telling her, in turn, about my parents and sister. Over the years since then my mother, Jan, and Marie have swopped family stories while Les and Gerry, our two fathers, have analysed cricket matches, and Ian's performances, over many a pint.

Somerset won this match and Ian appeared very shortly afterwards with glasses of champagne for us. It was certainly not a taste of things to come, as I rarely see him nowadays till hours after a match has finished.

As the cricket season drew to a close, I began to wonder what the winter would bring. Ian planned to work on a building site as he had no job other than cricket. I couldn't think of any good reason, business-wise, for travelling frequently the great distance to the West Country, so we had to content ourselves with telephone calls.

Ian, in company with many men, is not very good at ringing when he says he will. 'After all,' he used to say, 'you know I'm going to ring some time, it isn't always possible to ring exactly when I said I would.' But this wasn't good enough for me. I looked forward to his calls and hated it when he missed. I suppose I must have felt uncertain of him, although I had no reason to be, but as bedtime approached and the phone didn't ring I would become dejected and snappy. My family would sigh with relief when the call finally came through. I reckon I must have sensed then what an important part the telephone would play in our lives.

Towards the end of October, Mum and I travelled down to Somerset, she to stay with my uncle and aunt and me to stay for the weekend at Ian's home. By this time I had met his parents on several occasions and now I met his young brother, Graeme. I thought he was a super kid but in later months I became a little less enthusiastic when he insisted on accompanying us on our few precious times together. I used to drive Ian to matches with this eager nine-year-old standing in the back of the car, resting his arms on the back of our seats and joining in the conversation.

Les and Marie always made me welcome on my frequent visits to the West Country. Les had been an artificer in the Fleet Air Arm before leaving when Ian was five to take up an appointment with Westlands Helicopters which brought them to live in Yeovil. Marie was a busy housewife with four children of whom Ian is the eldest. During our chats over the washing-up I learned that I was the first girl Ian had taken home to meet his parents, also that when he wanted something he wasted no time in getting it.

Ian then, as now, needs to be surrounded by people.

ABOVE LEFT: Myself aged
18 months
ABOVE RIGHT: With my
younger sister Lindsay on
holiday in St Ives
LEFT: My first modelling
assignment – for a local
photographic society. I
was nine years old at the
time

ABOVE: Thorne Grammar School's
first eleven at hockey: myself third from
the right
ABOVE CENTRE: Mum and Dad as I first
remember them
ABOVE RIGHT: Engagement time at the
County Hotel, Taunton, 1975
RIGHT: A bright and frosty January day,
1976: Hallam Moseley to the left of Ian,
Brian Close and Pete ('Dasher') Denning
Sheffield Newspapers Ltd
BELOW: Our annual Easter Lake District
holiday with the Close family (Brian and
Viv and their two children)

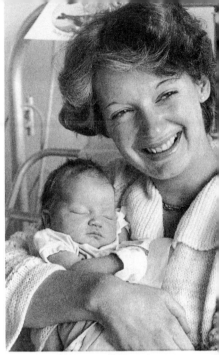

ABOVE LEFT: Birth of a
son, Liam
ABOVE RIGHT: Birth of a
daughter, Sarah: Ian was
on tour in Australia
RIGHT: Waiting at Lord's
for Ian's 100th Test
wicket (against India,
1979) *Patrick Eagar*

Even in these early days together he rarely felt the need to be alone with me – not often, anyway! Everywhere we went, his friends went too. Ian was only eighteen and the only one in a crowd of 'fellas' with a girlfriend. It was a relief when we made arrangements to meet Annie and Peter Denning. They were good friends and a foursome was so much nicer than a tensome, or a twelvesome, or even more.

So we were surrounded as usual at Carnaby's disco in Yeovil that weekend when Ian said, very matter-of-factly, 'I've decided. We're going to get married.' I laughed because he had had a bit too much to drink and I didn't really think that he meant it, nor was I sure that I wanted marriage at nineteen. It wasn't until the cold clear light of the next day that he assured me he had meant it. I don't really remember saying much except that I accepted.

We anticipated some opposition from our parents because of our age. I am the elder by six months, and we were eighteen and nineteen. I decided to broach the subject in the car on our way home. Mum was driving and when I mentioned that we were thinking of getting engaged, there was a moment's pause, a slight veering of the car towards the nearest hedge and a perceptible whitening of knuckles clutching the steering wheel.

Ian's father apparently was less passive about it: he laughed. He thought that we couldn't possibly be serious and, thinking back, I wonder how we could have been. Ian was an uncapped county player earning about £500 a year with no winter job. I was on a four-year polytechnic course with three years still to go.

Some days later Ian hitchhiked north to stay with me for a weekend. He saw quite a bit of the country as the lifts he got took him via Newcastle-under-Lyme and Manchester before Yorkshire. He arrived quite late and I had almost given him up, not knowing he was hitching lifts. I did wonder why he hadn't called asking me to meet him at the station.

I don't remember a great deal about that weekend except that he must have been delayed getting back because on the following Tuesday he rang to say that he had been sacked from the building site. Dad immediately suggested that he should come north again and work for him. We all thought this was an excellent idea. Ian had hit it off with my mother and father from day one and, for their part, my parents realized that this way we would have the chance to get to know each other and it would either make or break our relationship.

Ian had his nineteenth birthday shortly afterwards and as a present my parents gave him a course of driving lessons. Before long he was on the road selling drums and drumsticks for most of the week and driving me mad in the office for the rest of the time.

We had decided to announce our engagement at Christmas but we felt that one or two of our special friends should know first. Two of these were, of course, Brian and Vivienne Close. Although Ian would never admit it, we were both apprehensive about Closey's reaction. We might well have been for, when my parents told him at a dinner-dance they all attended, he hit the roof. Never one to hide his feelings, he hauled Mum and Dad over the coals for allowing it, thought of a thousand and one reasons why it shouldn't happen and generally grumbled and chuntered all evening.

I decided to get all the unpleasant bits over in one fell swoop and informed Mum and Dad that I had decided not to continue with my business studies course. I think they had been expecting it, for they didn't protest too much, and it was arranged that Ian and I should share a job and a half, he doing the selling in the winter and me in the summer, while during the winter months I would help with the trade shows and general administration.

We organized a party for our friends during which we planned to announce our engagement. The first to arrive were Brian and Viv. Brian marched in, the light of battle gleaming in his eye, shepherded us into the dining-room and firmly closed the door. 'Now then, listen here, you two bloody young fools.' It was a good beginning. He went on to warn and advise us of what was to come. I remember him saying, 'Ian is a bloody marvellous cricketer. He will play for England some day, Kathryn. You mustn't do anything to stop this. If you interfere with his career in any way I'll tan your arse. He must be single-minded and dedicated. You'll have to accept this.' To Ian he said, 'Kathryn is a wonderful girl. If you do anything to hurt her I'll skin you alive. Now go on – enjoy yourselves and remember what I've said.'

I do remember still. Then I thought of the times we'd had with the Closes: the good times, the people we'd met, the places we'd visited, the fun and laughter our two families had shared. I thought also of the not-so-good times: the headlines, losing the England captaincy, losing the Yorkshire captaincy, the times they had stayed with us to get away from the media. Does any of this sound familiar? At that time it was far from our young lives. We weren't even going to get married for at least another three years. At least, that's what we said then.

I quickly came to realize that life with Ian was quite definitely going to be incident-packed. On our visits to see Ian's parents I was filled in on his early years, his escapades as a schoolboy and his frequent visits to the casualty department at Yeovil general hospital. I was soon to become part of those visits which usually took place in the early hours of the morning because Ian always shrugged off injury when it happened, only to realize hours later that treatment was needed. A hand trapped in a car door, a finger broken in a football game, concussion from a cricket ball – all resulted in visits to hospital. I remember two things about Yeovil hospital – one was the very large file they had on Ian's earlier visits; I had always thought Marie had exaggerated in her stories but as the file almost needed two people to carry it I realized when I saw it that it was all true. The second was when I heard laughter coming from the cubicle in the emergency ward to which I had conveyed him at 4 a.m. and I discovered his injury was being dealt with by an ex-girlfriend. I was not amused. Come to think of it, it always seemed to be about 4 a.m. and I always seemed to be sitting on uncomfortable chairs listening to jokes and laughter from cubicles where Ian was being treated by nurses whom he was always able to charm. At least it stood me in good stead to deal with our son who, duly following his father's footsteps, has caused me to spend several winter evenings in the casualty department of Scunthorpe General where fishhooks have been extricated from his finger and various quite serious cuts, bumps and bruises have been dealt with.

Following our engagement and decision to wait three or four years before marriage, ten weeks later to be exact, we attended the wedding of a friend. During the wedding Ian announced that there was really no need for us to wait for years, we would get married at the end of that cricket season. In fact, we got married on 31 January of the following year, 1976.

Ian always makes snap decisions. He is always sure he is right, or manages to convince himself he is. Then he will set out to convince those around him, showing utter amazement if anyone disagrees with him. In these early days I usually allowed him to make the decisions even when I was not always sure it was the right thing to do. I have never enjoyed arguments (Ian will dispute this), and for the sake of harmony deferred to other people. Ian would often tell me that I had to stand up for myself and have more say in things generally. When I tried this, however, it was not always successful. These were early days, and I have changed over the years.

Ian's decision to get married then was welcomed by me and, in spite of everything, I have never seriously regretted it. Plans were made for the wedding and, again, I indulged my wish to please everyone at the expense of my own feelings. I would have liked a wedding with just one bridesmaid, my sister Lindsay. However, Lynn Close, who was nine at the time, was desperate to be a bridesmaid and I felt that Ian's family should be included. He has two sisters so I asked them both. Four bridesmaids! Oh well, everyone said it was a pretty wedding.

The next hurdle was, where were we going to live? I have always felt that the decision to live in the north did not go down well in certain quarters. Many people in Somerset felt that his loyalties should extend to living in the county for which he played. It was a logical decision however, as my permanent job was there as was Ian's winter job. We had made lots of friends and Ian loved it. He has the ability to settle quickly wherever he is, making friends easily and joining in any community. He played for a local football team and a very important consideration was that he relished the local beers. Again I received my instructions from him: 'Go and find us a house. I shall like anything you do.' Ian had made the big decision for us, to get married: now I carried out the 'minor' details.

We found a little cottage in Epworth, South Humber-side, which we bought for £7,950 – my parents gave us the deposit for a wedding present and we arranged a £30 per month mortgage. Not much by present-day standards but a small fortune to us then. Over the months before we were married Ian would send me his salary cheque to be put into a building society account and lived on his expenses. He never grumbled about this though there were

lapses when, for example, during pre-season training we
met in London when I was there on business. He
announced with glee that he had managed to get two
tickets for Chelsea (his team) versus Tottenham at White
Hart Lane. The tickets cost £12 each – I was livid. I didn't
like football at the best of times and think what we could
have done with £24!

In spite of our rigorous savings plan we enjoyed ourselves immensely in the run-up to our marriage. We didn't
feel trapped by lack of money as so many young couples
do. For a lot of the time Ian was living in hotels on
expenses and I was able to meet him there, having arranged
business trips to coincide with Somerset's fixture list – one
of the advantages of having a cricket-loving boss who
happened to be my father.

As many people know to their cost Ian is a practical
joker. Added to his enormous physical strength this can
be infuriating as you have absolutely no chance of retalia-
tion. He found uses for the ornamental pond in our garden
for which it was never intended, and Lindsay one day
found herself up to her knees in a fountain pool in London
after teasingly telling a group of his friends about the ballet
lessons he'd had as a child!

His fellow-cricketers were more often than not the
recipients of his 'humour' and were constantly plotting,
without much success, to get their own back. They did
notice, however, that when I was around Ian seemed to
become slightly less exuberant. One evening following a
Somerset/Derby game at Derby, we were having a quiet
meal together, just the two of us for a change, when
Lindsay, who had travelled to Derby with me, together
with some of Ian's team-mates, did a disappearing act from
the adjoining lounge on the pretext that they were going
out for a drink and would see us in about half an hour.
Later we set out for home whereupon Lindsay regaled me

with the events of their missing half-hour. Ian's hotel bedroom had been stripped of all furnishings which were neatly stacked in the bathroom. Even the base of the bed had gone and the television was on the balcony. A message was scrawled across the mirror in lipstick – a rude one I expect.

The next morning when he rang me I inquired solicitously whether he had had a good night's sleep! He asked to speak to Lindsay who, from the safe distance of fifty miles, owned up to being part of the prank.

The cricket season drew to a close. It hadn't been a particularly successful one. Ian had retained his place in the first eleven but had had to play a few second eleven games to gain practice. There was no sign as yet of the stardom that was to come and there was no way I could look forward to a secure future. At that time Brian Close was quoted as saying, 'He tried too hard to make things happen and they don't always happen in cricket.'

Ian returned north and resumed his job while we took possession of our little cottage in Epworth. Denis Breakwell, who had been a painter and decorator, offered to help us paint. Ian took a week off work and he and Denis disappeared every morning to Epworth with paint catalogues, dust cloths, brushes, etcetera. I was not allowed to go near it until it was finished, though I was consulted about colours. This was because he wanted to show me the finished product, I was told, but I strongly suspect it was because he knew I would object to the colossal mess they were making. However, the result was creditable, despite the fact that it took about two weeks to remove the paint splashes from the stone fireplace.

Ian revelled in this domesticity for a short time but then, as now, he felt he had to get away from it. A few business trips were organized and when Lindsay had to go to Durham University for an interview, Ian and I drove her there on the Sunday and Ian volunteered to return to pick her up the following day. He was most anxious that Lindsay shouldn't bother to come back on the train, he would be delighted to collect her, he said. This is the explanation behind the fact that Lindsay, in her smart interview outfit and high-heeled shoes, was standing in the middle of November on the terraces at Roker Park watching Sunderland play – and she hates football. She told us later that she had reluctantly agreed to go because Ian had bribed her with the promise of a meal afterwards. She didn't know at the time that it was to be a Chinese takeaway which she had to pay for.

During that autumn before our marriage there were times when Ian's actions mystified me. Why, for example, would anyone travel from Yorkshire to Somerset to play football on a Saturday afternoon for Ilminster Town, then return to play for Moorends Trinity in Yorkshire on Sunday? This he did on several occasions when the petrol money cost more than the expenses he was given. In 1985 he travelled to Yeovil from Epworth every Saturday to play for Yeovil Town, another decision I shall never understand.

Ian developed asthma during this football season. Each Tuesday evening he would go for training and return with a dry cough, looking dreadfully pale and out of breath. This worried us and we eventually persuaded him to see a doctor. The first doctor told him that as he found it difficult to get through a game of football without breathing difficulties, he had better give up sport. We arranged for a second opinion. In Doncaster he saw a respiratory specialist, and I can see his face now as he returned to the car where I was waiting, flung in a packet of cigarettes and said, 'I can forget about those – I've got asthma.' Following further tests he was found to be allergic to grass and exercise, just the job for a county cricketer. Thankfully he has never had a severe asthma attack and it hasn't really hampered his sport to any great extent, though there have been times when I know he hasn't been one hundred per cent fit. It is surprising how many top sportsmen do suffer from asthma.

As our wedding day approached we began hunting for bargains to furnish our little cottage. Being on a tight budget, December evenings found us fitting carpets, reorganizing the kitchen and hanging curtains. In the middle of all this the inevitable happened, another visit to Doncaster Royal Infirmary to have a plaster cast put on a fractured hand – a football injury. I became adept at wielding hammers and laying carpets and Ian was marvellous at sitting in an armchair giving instructions. Something he still excels at.

The plaster cast came off just in time for our wedding.

4

The County Season

I believe our wedding day went off without a hitch but, as happens to many young brides, I don't really remember a great deal about it.

We had planned a honeymoon in the Lake District and our answer to everyone who asked us how long we would be away was, 'As long as the money holds out.' We stayed away exactly four days.

We had a week's holiday so in the three days left to us we had plenty of time to unpack our wedding presents. Ian spent two days putting plugs on our various electrical appliances. It took two days, not because we had been given a vast amount of appliances but because he kept getting it wrong. Being of a practical nature I was more than capable of putting them on myself but there was no way that Ian was going to allow me to do this. I had to content myself with creeping into the kitchen to try the plugs, hoping against hope that we wouldn't be plunged into darkness.

Because of lack of money to pay for professional help, Ian and a friend decided to extend the central heating system upstairs. With strict instructions to stay away, I was packed off to my parents' house for the weekend. When Ian rang up to say it was working and that he would drive over to bring me home, he was terribly proud of himself. However, my feeling of unease grew as we journeyed home. 'It's really warm upstairs now,' he said. 'It wasn't as difficult a job as I thought. There's a bit of a mess but nothing that can't be put right. Of course, the pipes will need a coat of paint and there's a small hole in our bedroom floor and the dining-room ceiling, but apart from that everything's fine.'

It certainly was a lot warmer; in that respect he was quite right. The hole was almost big enough for me to crawl through and the house looked as though it had had twenty men working in it for a month.

Ian could never be called practical. At least in the early days he used to try, because there was no one else to do it, although Dad was always there to give a helping hand when permitted. Ian once said on television that he didn't help with changing the babies' nappies, implying he didn't believe in doing it because it's women's work. In fact, he is incapable of doing it. He tried it once and poor Liam ended up with the nappy draped in all the wrong places. I think he's frightened to try it again.

Shortly after our wedding it was my twenty-first birthday and Ian decided that we should have a party at home which he would arrange, enlisting Mum's help with the food. Friends and family came from Somerset bringing with them flagons of Scrumpy which friends from Epworth dismissed disdainfully as a 'cissy' drink. By 10 p.m. there were half-stupefied bodies all over the place while the Somerset contingent partied on.

April brought the beginning of the 1976 cricket season and Ian had to return to Somerset for pre-season training. The harsher realities of life with an absent husband made themselves felt. It was more than that, though. We both realized that it was to be a make-or-break year. If Ian was going to make his way in life as a cricketer he had to begin now. If not, decisions about our future would have to be made. I used to listen anxiously to the lunchtime scoreboard and scan the newspapers for Ian's name, revelling in his success and feeling cast down if he was less than successful.

As often as possible I would go to Taunton at weekends and stay at the County CC flat near the ground. It was a dreadful place. I tried to cook meals in saucepans without handles and going to the loo was rather like entering an obstacle race – you had to take a large bowl of water with you to flush it. Ian would invite people in for meals and, as I hated anything to be less than perfect, I would spent hours tidying things up and planning and cooking. They were certainly not very relaxing weekends. I had a friend who was a nurse in Taunton who used to smuggle me into the nurses' home to have a bath, the bathroom at the flat being completely impossible. We would return to the flat in our dressing-gowns – by car of course. This was all right until one evening the car wouldn't start outside the nurses' home. We were pushed by a group of boys. Goodness knows what they thought.

When I returned on Sundays to our home in Epworth, I never knew exactly when I would see Ian again. I couldn't adjust to this and resented it even more because Ian apparently accepted it quite happily. Looking back I now realize that this was all part of his character: wherever he was and whatever circumstances prevailed, he went along with them. He didn't allow things to get on top of him and worrying didn't seem to be part of his make-up.

In stark contrast to this, although not necessarily wanting to be the leader I did want to be in control of my life and needed to know what was in store, for at least a few months ahead. During the week I would spend the days at work and the evenings working around the house, then juggle with accounts trying to make ends meet. I had no one to discuss household problems with, so many of them became insurmountable in my mind. I looked forward to

the times when I was able to meet Ian, and the troubles
would lift. We would spend most of our time together
happily but as the time to leave drew near worries would
begin to creep back into my mind and I would think of all
the things I should be discussing with my husband, even
though I was aware he just wouldn't want to know about
them. I would grow quiet and pensive and he would
become irritated with me, 'What's the matter with you?'
'Nothing,' was my stock answer. I always carried Brian's
warning with me. Nothing must stop Ian from realizing
his ambitions. Therefore, I mustn't worry him. What a
fool I was! I should have realized that very little worried
Ian. One of his most striking attributes is his confidence,
and he was always confident that things would work out
all right in the end.

I would go home and become more and more dejected
as I tried to make our money stretch to cover mortgage,
heating bills and the unexpected expenses that always
seemed to crop up when I least wanted them. I tried hard
during telephone calls not to let Ian realize my moods, but
he must have sensed my feelings because sometimes he
would bring other people to the phone with the intention
of cheering me up. In fact this would have the opposite
effect. Frequently, the calls would come on benefit nights,
and from other wives who were there with their husbands.
(Players awarded benefit years make money by organizing,
among other things, social events at which other players
and their wives are present.) This would make me feel that
not only did I want to be there but that I should be there.
I would put the phone down and wonder if we were doing
the right thing by living in the north; should we think
about moving down to the West Country?

The answer was always, 'What kind of work could I
get?' or 'What would Ian do in the winter?' Many of the
Somerset players spent their winters on the dole. My

depression was not helped by the fact that newspapers began to carry stories saying that younger members of the Somerset County Cricket Club were unhappy with Brian Close as their captain, and that he was too harsh with them. Ian certainly, during that season, had had his ups and downs with Brian. I feel, however, that certain senior members within the side were becoming jealous of Brian's successful leadership which was turning Somerset into a winning team. They were the ones who were stirring up dissatisfaction among the younger players, Ian in particular. For a time things became rather strained but thankfully neither Ian nor Brian was foolish enough to let it affect their relationship permanently.

In any event they were able to talk things over in privacy because, following our marriage, Closey had decided that Ian should travel to away matches with him to the relief of other players who had hitherto taken their turn in his passenger seat. It never ceased to amaze Ian that Brian would make cups of tea on the journeys with the help of a little gadget which plugged into the cigarette lighter. Presumably this was intended for use in lay-bys but Brian scorned this refinement. He would also make considerable detours to pick up a copy of the *Sporting Life* and then proceed to read it in snatches as though map-reading while driving to the ground. It has been known for Ian to steer the car from the passenger seat to enable Brian to turn over the pages. He wears an expression of injured innocence these days when reminded of this and also appears to suffer from loss of memory.

It was during this season that Ian was awarded his county cap, a reward for his cricketing performances. Luckily I was at the match where this occurred. We had been spending the weekend with Les and Marie Botham and I remember Marie and I straining to catch a glimpse of the award. Not only was it cheerful news for Ian but it was welcome news to his accountant in Epworth, namely me, as his pay cheque was more than doubled.

Things did begin to look a little more cheerful now. Ian's cricket was going well and newspapers began to talk of him being chosen to play for England. Discussions about leaving me behind to coach abroad for the winter subsided, and a few days free from cricket saw us on our way, just the two of us, for a short holiday in Scotland, arranged as a surprise for me. Only Ian with just three days' holiday would have thought of travelling to Yorkshire immediately after a cricket match – cadging a lift with Closey – to pick me up, setting off again in the early hours of the morning to travel to Loch Ness. We had a super time, though, finding little bed-and-breakfast places, and I luxuriated in the unaccustomed privacy and solitude.

We raced back home to Epworth. Ian had to take the car to get back to Taunton. I was able to arrange some business in London the following week and went down to collect it from Lord's where Somerset were playing Middlesex.

Some time previously the old Austin 1100 had been replaced by a smart new Ford Escort. It was the firm's car, of course, but I was lucky enough to have more or less the sole use of it with Ian taking over whenever possible. Originally not very keen to learn to drive, he now loved it and drove fast and furiously as you would expect. By the time the car was sold the only original parts were the bonnet and the passenger door.

This particular weekend in London it was the turn of the boot. I picked him up from Lord's at the end of the match and had been allowed to park the car inside the ground. Ian came along with the inevitable friend and they both cheerfully tossed their cricket gear into the boot.

'Right,' said Ian. 'Off we go,' and we did – backwards, straight into a tree. There was a moment's silence. I was stricken: we'd got the car back from the garage only a few days before the Scotland trip. Inspecting the damage we found that a large plane tree now seemed to be part of the car. The boot was caved inwards and the bumper was lovingly wrapped around the tree trunk. 'Don't worry,' said Ian cheerfully, 'it will soon knock out!'

Throughout the remainder of that evening I rehearsed the way I was going to break the news to Dad. Ian didn't really seem to think about it at all but I did notice that he was good at inventing reasons why it would be better not to telephone and make our confessions that evening.

The next morning I picked up the telephone and handed it to him. 'You did it, you confess,' I insisted. He dialled the number and I heard him say 'Now then, T.G., are you in a good mood? Right then. You see, it was like this. There's this tree at Lord's . . .' It was after this I believe that my father – Thomas Gerald – became known as T.G. – so christened by Ian in a fit of bravado.

Several years later, in one of the first books about Ian, Dudley Doust wrote, 'Travelling in a battered car, Ian . . .' My father was outraged. 'It was only battered after Ian had had it a few months,' he said. 'What a liberty!'

Much to my father's relief, it was about this time that we decided we really must have a car of our own which Ian could use regularly. Ian was delighted with his first car and it made our lives easier as whenever he was playing near enough he would get special permission from the club and come home for the evening.

When Somerset played Nottingham at Trent Bridge he brought Denis Breakwell and Hallam Moseley home for the weekend. They set off on the Sunday morning to report for duty in the John Player League match. As they arrived at Trent Bridge the gateman stopped the car and Ian wound the window down. 'Somerset players.'

'Oh no you're not,' came the reply. Ian was a little taken

aback. Not being the most patient of people he snapped back, 'What the – do you mean? The three of us are playing for Somerset. Here! Today! I am Ian Botham, this is Denis Breakwell and this is Hallam Moseley.'

Unmoved, the gateman replied, 'Mr Close has told me that all the Somerset team have arrived.'

With that, both passengers got out of the car, towering over the little gateman, and opened the gate themselves. Ian drove through and parked the car while the gateman disappeared into the distance having issued a threat: 'I've a son bigger than you – I'll fetch him along to sort you all out.'

When I arrived later with Marcia Moseley and baby the gateman, obviously having checked on Ian and now wishing to put things right, was most helpful and rushed to find us a parking space. Commenting on this at the end of the match brought somewhat unresponsive grunts from Ian, Denis and Hallam.

On the following day, in the county championship match, Ian scored his maiden century, 167 not out. This caught the eye of the selectors and he was chosen for the Prudential one-day series against the West Indies.

The whole family turned out to support him and the start of the match found us all at Scarborough waiting nervously. I wish I had a pound for every hour I have spent waiting nervously since then. Believe me, it doesn't become any easier as time goes on. There is really not much to say about that match. Ian was singularly unsuccessful: he was out for one and his bowling took a bit of a hammering.

With the invitation to play for England comes a long list of 'dos' and 'don'ts' with regard to dress and behaviour, and it still does eleven years later. Ian obeyed these to the letter. This may surprise people as he has always been portrayed as the rebel. This was his first appearance for

England and I was soon to realize that Ian's cricketing life was very much separate from his family life. Rightly or wrongly he just didn't want me with him. For a period of about a week while he travelled with the Prudential squad he ate, breathed and slept English cricket. I had no part in it and felt very much the outsider. It was a difficult position for me, as though Ian's life was becoming a jigsaw and I was the odd piece that didn't seem to fit in anywhere. I would like to be able to say that I understood this, but I didn't and I resented it deeply. Throughout this season I had longed for Ian to be chosen to represent his country and now it had happened where had it left me? There was no answer. From the maturity of my thirty-odd years I would deal with the situation very differently now, but then so would Ian. As it was I grew quieter and sulked and Ian didn't even seem to notice, which made me even more annoyed. Although his international début had been a bit of a disaster, Ian had been assured by the captain, Tony Greig, that he wanted him in the squad to tour India that winter, 1976–7. Ian's spirits were buoyant and he was looking forward to playing for England in India. Two weeks later, as I was working in Cheltenham, I heard the touring team announced on Radio 2's Sportsdesk. Ian was not in it. I felt that he would be shaken by the news but in actual fact, by the time I saw him, he was fine and although he must have been hurt it didn't show. Looking back, the selectors were wrong to pick him for the one-day matches at the end of the season, and against the West Indies of all people.

After the last match of that summer our lives took on a semblance of normality. I actually had a husband who went out to work in the morning and came home in the evening and who was at home to take part in social occasions. We had just acquired a boxer puppy which was intended as a consolation for Ian having to spend the winter at home. I drew up very strict rules: to bed in the kitchen, no dogs upstairs, etcetera. Why then did Ian's first night home with Tigger end up with us sleeping rigidly at each side of the bed with a seven-week-old puppy curled up between us snuffling blissfully?

Although I love dogs, they do tend to become the bane of my life. These days we have two at a time and the larger the better. Tigger had been a surprise gift for Ian and he was delighted. Years later he returned the compliment by giving me a great dane puppy for Christmas. I was horrified.

In late October the touring party flew off to India and Ian immediately became easier to live with, as he was able to put the possibility of going out of his mind. In November his twenty-first birthday came and went, not altogether uneventfully. We had spent Ian's twenty-first at his parents' home in Yeovil and several of our close friends from Epworth had travelled to Somerset. We were all having elevenses when suddenly a heated exchange issued from the dining-room where Ian, his sister Dale and their father were talking. At the time Dale was a nursing student doing an SRN course at Wythenshaw Hospital. She had recently become the proud owner of her first car and had foolishly asked Ian if he would like to try it out and see what he thought of it. It became increasingly obvious to us that the comments he was making were not to Dale's liking and in typical brother and sisterly fashion a slanging match occurred. I see history repeating itself so often in my own children's relationships.

Marie self-consciously got up to try and pour oil on what were becoming very troubled waters. She was unsuccessful and the conversation became even more heated. The coffee-drinkers in the lounge, who included me, were busily trying to pretend it wasn't happening, but we couldn't ignore the next line as Ian flung open the dining-room door and as a parting shot asked Dale, 'Are you sure it's not two halves stuck together?' He then walked through to join us, picking up the threads of our conversation as though nothing had happened. Dale could be heard sobbing noisily, comforted by Marie. This is typical of Ian, causing a furore and then settling down in the middle of it as though nothing unusual is happening.

We intended that our first Christmas in our new home would be a traditional family one. My own parents and sister lived nearby and we invited Marie, Les and Ian's two sisters and young brother to stay with us over the Christmas period. This was the first and last time that Ian and I ever went Christmas shopping together. Ian finds it a complete and utter bore. He has never forgotten the occasion when he went with me to buy my wedding shoes. We saw the pair I eventually bought in the first shop we visited in Sheffield. In between we went to Doncaster and Leeds, returning to Sheffield the following week. I don't think I have yet been fully forgiven for that. Christmas shopping on a limited budget nearly finished him off. I love to match the present to the person and find pleasure in searching for the right gift. Ian is a five o'clock Christmas Eve shopper, homing in on whatever might be remotely suitable at whatever the cost.

This first Christmas I wanted to be perfect and I was prepared to spend a lot of time making it so. We busied ourselves buying a Christmas tree and decorating the house. I made my own cake, pudding, mince-pies and all the traditional goodies. Then the blow fell, only a few days before Christmas. Donald Carr, the then secretary of the Test and County Cricket Board, telephoned to inform Ian that he had been selected for the Whitbread scholarship scheme. It was the first time it had been in operation and, along with Bill Athey, Mike Gatting and Graham Stevenson, Ian was to spend three months as from the 3rd of January in Australia.

Ian was thrilled. I was devastated. The last three months I had learned what it was like to live as a married couple – together. What was to have been a peaceful and happy family Christmas now revolved round preparations for Ian's departure.

What with Ian's excitement and my misery, the financial aspect had not occurred to us. The scholarship did not make provision for wives at home; expenses and living accommodation in Australia were provided only for the players. When we finally did think about this, Ian rang up and reminded Mr Carr that he was married and had the usual domestic expenses to take care of. Several telephone calls later we were informed that the sponsors would pay me £100 a month. We appreciated this very much because we fully realized that they could very easily have selected someone else instead. In theory this sum, together with my salary, meant we could manage: in practice, it didn't work that way.

However, I tried to put all these problems behind me as Ian's family arrived on Christmas Eve. Our little two-bedroomed cottage bulged at the seams and we had put-u-up beds all over the place. During preparations for Christmas dinner I began to feel vaguely unwell, 'Flu', I thought, 'what an inconvenient time to be ill.' Ian's mother is marvellous in times of crisis, and she quickly realized I needed help, although I had planned to do everything myself to give both mothers a complete rest. During the pudding course I had to retire to bed and lay there listening to the festivities going on below.

At first Ian was sympathetic to my pleas for peace and a rest from the television and radio which seemed to be blaring out at odds with each other in the rooms below. I struggled to get through the Christmas period and then returned to work only to spend most of my first day back at my parents' home in bed. Feeling so wretched all the time, I became very snappy and quick to find fault. Really, I just wanted to be left alone.

Marie and Les, with the best intentions in the world, decided to stay on longer, thinking I needed help. In fact, this was just what I did not need. Ian had only a few days left at home and I wanted there to be just the two of us. The house no longer seemed to be ours and Ian and I, both edgy because of his imminent departure, spent too much time falling out over trivial things in heated whispers.

I roused myself sufficiently to accompany Ian to the airport to say goodbye. This was the first and only time I have seen Ian off at an airport. I returned home feeling sick and miserable, realizing that 1977 had not begun in a very propitious way.

5

Botham for England – and Birth of a Son

I spent the next day or two turning recent events over in my mind. It had all seemed such a rush, there were a thousand and one things I had wanted to say, lots of things we had planned to do together and now the opportunity was gone. I didn't even know Ian's address; that was to be fixed up when he arrived.

At the back of my mind was the possibility of pregnancy. When the flu symptoms had not given way to the expected heavy cold, I began to think that the tension caused by Ian's impending departure and the constant presence of so many people had made me feel off-colour. Ian had said, without any real conviction and almost as a joke, 'Well, you could be pregnant,' but the events of the moment had overshadowed everything else and neither of us had really seriously considered it. Mum arrived one evening shortly after Ian's departure, determined to get me to eat. She offered to make anything I fancied and I replied, 'The only thing I fancy is porridge.' Even then, when she looked at me knowingly and said, 'I think I may know what's wrong with you – have you thought you may be pregnant?', I just smiled and returned the thought to the back of my mind. (Mum told me later that before I was born the only thing she could eat was porridge.)

Eventually I decided to consult a doctor, and five days

after Ian had gone I learnt that I was indeed pregnant. Of course, I wanted to tell someone but it couldn't be Ian because I still didn't know where he was, except that he was somewhere in Melbourne, Australia, twelve thousand miles away. I drove to Thorne to tell my parents who were absolutely delighted, though not at all surprised. Dad opened a bottle of champagne and we sat around discussing how we could let Ian know as soon as possible. I was absolutely determined that no one else should know before he did.

I rang Lord's and they didn't know where he was staying but suggested that I should contact Colin Cowdrey, who had co-ordinated the arrangements for the Whitbread scholarship scheme. I was very concerned not to make a fuss. We had already asked for financial help over and above the scholarship and I certainly didn't want anyone to think I was the anxious little wife checking up on her husband's whereabouts.

I tentatively rang the number and spoke to Colin who was very helpful. He said that he didn't yet know where Ian was staying but he did know a number where he thought I would be able to contact him. He offered to ring the number himself and let me know. Within a few minutes he had returned my call and said, 'Ian is staying with Frank Tyson at the moment, but this isn't to be his permanent address. However, I have arranged that he will ring you within the next half-hour.' I was very grateful for his help, particularly as he hadn't asked the reason for my wanting to get in touch.

I sat eagerly waiting for the telephone to ring. I learnt later that Ian had been out when Colin had rung and Frank Tyson, the former England fast bowler now living in Australia, had immediately set about finding him. I didn't have to wait long before I could tell an anxious Ian the news. I waited for his reaction, and waited, and waited.

Eventually he spoke, absolutely thrilled and excited but, for once, unable to find the words to express himself.

Returning to the champagne I felt so much better. I phoned Les and Marie and told them. They were also delighted: it was to be the first grandchild for both sets of parents, and there was so much for us all to look forward to.

I think it was Mum who suggested that it would be a good idea to ring Colin Cowdrey and tell him why I had so urgently wanted to contact Ian. He was pleased I had rung and said what wonderful news it was.

Following the euphoria, coming back to the harsher realities of life was a blow. For the next six weeks I spent much of the time feeling absolutely dreadful. As any mum who has suffered in this way will know, the feeling is indescribable. I continued to go to work, needing both the money and the company, but I didn't get much work done. Nor did Sandra, one of the girls in the factory, who spent most of her time driving me back to my parents' home to be put to bed, my complexion a ghastly shade of green. I vividly remember trying hurriedly to type a letter in the office one day while Dad was on the telephone to Germany. Like the Incredible Hulk I started to go green and a buzzing in my ears intensified then receded, and I dimly heard, 'Just a minute, Fritz. Are you all right, Tink?' I slumped in my chair unable to answer. As I was coming round I heard him saying calmly, 'I'll have to ring back, Fritz, Kathryn's just fainted.'

Ian rang frequently to ask how I was and each time inquired whether I had a 'bump' yet. They were always transfer-charge calls which even I didn't consider as I was pleased to be able to talk to him. That is, until I saw the telephone bill which consumed the whole of one month's allowance!

I spent hours in the evenings trying to make our money

stretch, but as most people know it just isn't elastic. Ian was not having too good a time in Australia cricket-wise and, ever mindful of my role as efficient, supportive wife in the background, I didn't tell him of the difficulties I was having. At a recent dinner in Adelaide Ian was asked about these early days in Australia. His reply was, 'I notched up a few centuries, unfortunately not as a batsman. I didn't trouble the scorer too much.'

While Ian was having little success in notching up runs or wickets in Melbourne, I was having great success in notching up bills in Epworth. I worry a great deal, working on the premise that if I worry about something it won't happen. So it follows that I'm worried if I've nothing to worry about, if you see what I mean. Ian doesn't believe in worrying. He says, 'Worry when it happens, if you worry before it happens you only worry twice.' However, this time my philosophy worked for me pretty well, as Dad decided I deserved a hefty pay rise, back-dated, to celebrate the fact that I no longer spent most of my working life in bed.

Through my work in the music industry I had come to know Carl and Maureen Palmer of the group Emerson, Lake and Palmer. I contacted Maureen to say that I was coming to London to meet Ian on his return from Australia and was immediately invited to stay overnight together with Angie, Graham Stevenson's wife. When we arrived at Maureen's we were greeted with the news that Ian and Graham had been delayed. The next day brought a further telephone call from Ian to say that he had been invited to play in an Invitation England XI in New Zealand, an opportunity we both agreed was too good to miss. Maureen immediately suggested that I stay on with her and we went shopping together. I remember buying a dress specially to meet Ian which I could really ill-afford.

I set off for the airport in my new dress, only to find a

thirteen-hour delay on the flight caused by engine trouble at Bombay. It was an early lesson in the wisdom of ringing for flight information before setting out to meet a plane. During my thirteen-hour wait I had more than enough time to envisage our romantic reunion. In reality it wasn't at all as I had imagined. Ian was very tired from a long-haul flight plus delay, very concerned about the fact that his luggage had been badly damaged and more than a little dismayed that at four months I didn't look at all pregnant. I think he thought it was all a myth. When I had assured him that it was indeed fact he immediately became very protective. I wasn't even allowed to carry the duty-free and, under no circumstances would he let me drive, even part of the way home. This proved to be a big mistake as he soon realized, surveying the damage to the front incurred by sliding on black ice into the rear end of a Ford Escort at a roundabout on the A1. The driver of the other car was most understanding.

With more to occupy my mind, this second year of marriage was much happier. I had adjusted to life on my own and was beginning to enjoy my independence. Ian had begun the 1977 season well and his good form was to continue. He was happy, too, and we both looked forward to the arrival of our first child.

A young couple, Julie and Bob, had moved into the farmhouse next door. Bob was an avid Scunthorpe United follower which meant that Julie was also left on her own at times. We became firm friends and had great fun together. Bob was always ready to help me catch the odd mouse which occasionally sheltered in our house. We were getting to know more people in the village and I would often find vegetables left on my doorstep. Bob's father Jack was a keen cricket follower and was ever ready with advice for Ian on his visits home.

During the Bath Festival in the early part of the season,

Somerset played the touring Australians and, as I always did when Ian was with Somerset, I travelled down for the long weekend of the match. There was quite a bit of media interest in Ian and he was being tipped to play for England quite soon. He was twenty-one and hailed as the greatest English all-round prospect since W. G. Grace. I was proud and delighted when I read these reports, and also very naive about the workings of the press. I didn't realize then that this premature build-up puts such an enormous amount of pressure on players, to the extent that many are broken rather than made by it.

It was here also that I was initiated into the irritation of having to sit passively while behind me unknown people were discussing my husband. Two such 'gentlemen' sat behind me in Bath.

'What do you think of this fellow Botham?'

'Oh, he's pretty good. I've seen him play a game or two.'

'Do you think he'll make it for England?'

'I'd think so, he's highly thought of around here.'

'Oh, I don't know. I think I'd put my money on Roebuck: Cambridge you know, the right calibre.'

These two must have often wondered why they were treated to such a withering glance from the young lady in front of them. My famous 'look' comes in very handy sometimes. In addition, I was gratified that Ian did so well in this match. He took the first catch of the match and proceeded to take five wickets, then followed this with innings of 59 (including three sixes) and 39 not out.

In the next few weeks the first and second Test matches were played without Ian being chosen. I don't remember him being disappointed, however. I think by now he was supremely confident that his inclusion would come eventually.

Late in the evening on Saturday 23 July, Ian's mother

rang. 'Isn't it wonderful news about Ian?' she said.

'What news?' I asked.

'Oh!' There was a long silence. 'I'm sorry, Kathryn, I thought you would know by now that Ian has been chosen for the next Test. We had a celebratory drink with him after the game at the ground and we've been home a while. I was sure he would have rung you by now.'

I was absolutely livid. When he did eventually ring to tell me, I was icy cold and distinctly lacking in enthusiasm. 'I already know. Perhaps next time you have something marvellous to tell me I may be among the first few to be informed!' – adding sarcastically, 'although I do realize I'm only your wife.' I was really thrilled, though, and soon the ice thawed and we were talking eagerly, making plans for the next few days.

The third Test match was at Nottingham, not far from our home, so Marie and Les arranged to come to stay with us. I was amused by the number of phone calls from long-lost distant relations and friends: 'We haven't seen you for ages. Just ringing to say we must get together some time. Oh, by the way, I don't suppose there is any chance of a ticket for the Test match?' The allocation of Test match tickets, then as now, is four complimentary ones per day, extra to be paid for. Over the next few years Ian juggled with tickets and days and people, trying to please everyone and often ending up buying quite a few.

People always seemed to ask me rather than Ian. 'I don't want to bother Ian,' they would say, but it was I who would then have to bother Ian, risking his displeasure when I asked for too many tickets. Ian really needs to think of the match ahead instead of dashing around on the opening day of a Test match trying to find extra tickets, so now I have learned to say, 'I'll tell you what, Ian's staying at —, if you contact him there he'll tell you whether there are any spare.' More often than not people don't bother.

The Test and County Cricket Board followed up their invitation to play with an official letter, 'Conditions of Acceptance and Notes and Instructions for Test Matches'. It was a large document containing sixteen clauses, relating to numerous provisions expected and unexpected. Among them we were informed that the playing fees were £210 per match per cricketer, £116 for twelfth man on duty throughout the match. Ian's big toes were to be insured for £1,600 each and his others £600 each. His life, if taken on duty, was worth £30,000. Clothing: all cricketers were to be issued with a cap, a tie, a blazer, a sleeveless and a long-sleeved sweater. A new blazer may only be issued to a cricketer who has been playing for England for over eight years. I was very proud when I saw him with the three lions of England on his chest, although those sweaters have since given me nightmares – like the time they all came out of the wash a delicate pink and I had to ring up Lord's and confess.

The first day of the Test match dawned bright and clear. Five of us – both sets of parents and myself – set off for Trent Bridge. Les, unusually, elected to drive. I am sure we were all more nervous than Ian. Les seemed to be having difficulty in recognizing colours as he drove straight through all the red lights and waited an agonizingly long time at the green ones, unperturbed by the angry motorists behind. We had to park a long way from the entrance to the ground and by the time we reached our seats a combination of nerves and breathlessness from hurrying while extremely pregnant caused a few anxious glances to be made in my direction.

It was a super day. After a ropey beginning Ian did well, ending the day with five wickets. It was royal jubilee year. The Queen visited the ground and Ian was introduced to her along with the other members of the team. We were thrilled by the fact that she went on, after the introduction, to have a few words with him, telling him that she had heard he had been doing some hard work.

At the end of the day many people came up to say how well Ian had played, asking us to pass on congratulations. Ray Illingworth, whom we had known for several years, passed us, with his wife Shirley. He stopped and said, 'Give Ian my congratulations but tell him it won't always be so easy. He's got a lot for a few today, tomorrow it will be none for many.' I have never forgotten those words or the way they were spoken. On the face of it they were congratulatory, but I felt then they were caustic and introduced a sour note. I have never changed my opinion. Throughout Ian's career to date, Raymond Illingworth has been his biggest critic. Fair criticism he can take and Ian has never minded any sports writer taking him to task for mistakes and poor performances, but the criticism levelled at him by Mr Illingworth has consistently been vindictive and hurtful. Together with Denis Compton he has written to the effect that Botham is not a great cricketer and never has been. In the *Sunday Mirror* prior to the Headingley Test Match of 1981 Illingworth wrote: 'Ian Botham is over-rated, over-weight and over-paid. He should be dropped from the team.' Ian scored 50 and 149 not out and took six wickets in the first innings. His 149 was hit after England had followed on, 227 runs behind, and were already five wickets down in their second innings.

I have found it significant that both Denis Compton and Ray Illingworth were former great English sportsmen. Ian is now reputed to be the greatest English all-rounder ever. Could the words of Louis St Just be appropriate? 'Jealous mediocrity will ever wish to bring genius to the scaffold' (although there was nothing mediocre about Compton's talent as a cricketer).

While I was talking to Ray Illingworth during that Nottingham Test match, Ian was doing several television and radio interviews. In the course of one of these he stated, 'My wife was eight months pregnant at the start of this match and I hope she still is!' This went down in print as a quote of the year.

The next Test match was at Headingley on 11 August. I really can't remember much about it except that he played well again, taking five wickets in an innings, and that on the fourth day just prior to an England win he stepped awkwardly on the ball when fielding and had to retire injured. The injury turned out to be a march fracture of a metatarsal bone of the left foot. It finished his cricket for the rest of the season and at the same time made it possible for him to be with me when Liam was born on 26 August.

Because we had expected Ian to be playing cricket around the date of the baby's arrival we had not planned that he would be present at the birth. I had moved in with Mum and Dad in case the baby announced its arrival in the middle of the night.

It was indeed the middle of the night when things began to happen and in the early hours of Thursday the 25th, Ian drove his British Leyland sponsored car, a red TR7, to Doncaster Royal Infirmary announcing as we went through the front door, 'I shan't be long. I'm not stopping.'

In the event he hardly left my side, except when told by the Sister on duty to go and rest and she invited him into her office for a cigarette. He applied himself fully to the job of being by my side with that single-mindedness that marks everything he does, and he was a tremendous help. At 3.50 a.m. on 26 August Liam was born, a very healthy 8lb 10oz.

On the following Sunday, the 28th, there was to be a presentation at Taunton to Brian Close who had announced his retirement from first-class cricket on the day Ian played in his first Test match at Trent Bridge. Ian

The Bothams in Australia, January 1980

ABOVE: Keeping it in the
family: Ian congratulates
my sister Lindsay on her
wedding-day
LEFT: Liam meets the
'Incredible Hulk' in
California

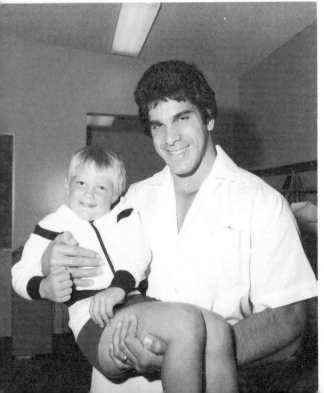

RIGHT: Antigua: facing up to
the press (1986) *Press
Association*
BELOW: One libel action
quashed: now for some lunch!
Press Association

LEFT: A rare, cricket-free holiday in the south of France (1983)
BELOW: A familiar role: Ian away, our third child Becky present
Daily Mirror

certainly wished to be at the presentation, as did Dad, so they planned to go to Taunton and back on the Sunday. Ian visited me at husbands' visiting hour – 8.30 a.m. – then he and Dad zoomed to Taunton in record time and were back to visit me again at 6.30 p.m.!

Two very proud parents left the maternity hospital with their six-day-old son and returned to Epworth to begin life as a threesome.

Ian's foot gradually healed and he was pronounced fit enough to be selected for the Pakistan/New Zealand tour which was to begin on 24 November, his birthday. I hated the thought of him going away and, as tour has followed tour, the weeks prior to his departure haven't become any easier. Everything revolves round thoughts of the tour. The team is selected and the invitation arrives, together with the inevitable rules and regulations and contract. Hat size, chest size, waist measurement, inside leg, have to be entered on numerous forms and sent to various places. I'm not sure why, because Ian's touring clothes have never yet fitted him or been anything like the sizes returned – this has given us a few laughs over the years. The last tour of Australia saw Ian arriving there without any touring clothes, as those provided would have needed two Joel Garners to fill them out.

There is also always a medical, which used to take place in London. This first tour Ian planned to travel to the medical with the Derbyshire fast bowler Mike Hendrick, while his wife Kathleen and I spent the day together.

I tucked Liam into his carrycot at about six-thirty and shortly afterwards Kath said goodnight to her young ones. She then produced a bottle of sherry and said, 'No doubt the boys will have drunk the train dry. We might as well have a drink.' They arrived back at about eight stone-cold sober because there had not been a buffet car on the train, while we had had rather too many sherries. Thankfully we were thought to be very amusing. For years Mike would remind me of that evening.

An England cricketer preparing to go on tour can well be compared with a child going off to boarding school. Included on the long list of instructions and suggestions is the recommendation that all items should be marked with the player's name. As is my nature, I took this literally and settled down to sew name tags on to shirts, socks, trousers, underpants, etcetera. As is Ian's nature, he left the trying-on of tour clothing until the last minute so the evening before his departure I found myself sitting in front of a mountain of cricket trousers and touring trousers to be shortened. I detest sewing at the best of times; I know that whatever I do doesn't last very long and safety-pins have played a large part in Ian's preparation for matches. Subsequent tours found me wielding a laundry-marker rather than a needle and cotton and in recent years I just haven't bothered.

Because of my previous experience in seeing Ian off at Heathrow I decided that this time I didn't want to go. As soon as Ian sets off to do anything he becomes part of it to the exclusion of everything else. As the players gather together the tour immediately gains momentum and I personally feel that it is not a place for wives. In any case, I prefer to say my goodbyes in private.

It was impossible to travel by train with the vast amount of luggage required so my father was prevailed upon to drive Ian to the meeting place at Lord's. This became a ritual and Ian now expects that, whoever is driving him, Dad will accompany them. Dad told me that whenever he set off with Ian for a tour the first half of the journey would be made in absolute silence while it was obvious that Ian was brooding over the people and things he had left behind. Then, quite suddenly, the silence would be broken and the banter would begin. As far as Ian was concerned the tour had started, and that now would be uppermost in his mind.

Ken Barrington was England's assistant manager at this time and he and Ian shared the same birthday. On the plane going over a birthday cake had been provided and I believe they had quite a good party. It was on this tour that Ian and Ken developed a strong bond. Ken was a good listener and was always ready to help in any way that was needed. Ian has always said of Ken that he was one of the very few 'old' cricketers who didn't harp back to their days on the field of play; he realized that cricket as played today demands much more of its players and he didn't mind admitting it. They developed a relationship similar to that of father and son, with the inherent respect for each other that such a relationship demands if it's to be successful. I know that Ken's death during Ian's subsequent reign as captain in the West Indies in 1981 left an unfillable gap. Recently in Australia Ian was asked who had had the most influence on his cricketing life – without hesitation he named Ken. On the same tour Meg Simpson, wife of the former Australian captain Bobby Simpson, told me that Ken, or 'the Colonel' as Ian nicknamed him, and his wife Ann were very close to Ian. I still keep in contact with Ann and during the difficult periods of our life she has always supported us with reassuring words.

On this 1977–78 tour of Pakistan and New Zealand the all-rounder spot in the team was fought out between Mike Gatting and Ian, and at first Mike was preferred. This meant that Ian played very little cricket in Pakistan which was the first port of call.

Back at home I had returned to work part-time and in between feeds my grandmother, fondly known as G.G. by her great-grandchildren, kept an eye on Liam.

It was only a matter of days after Ian's arrival in Pakistan that I received a message by courtesy of the BBC which simply stated: 'Ring Ian urgently – day or night – it's a matter of life or death.' I tried for several hours to get through to Pakistan, but the lines were constantly engaged. In the end I rang back Peter Baxter, the BBC's sports producer in London, who had relayed the message to me and, again courtesy of the BBC, he offered to contact Ian and tell him the situation. Eventually, some hours later, Ian was able to phone me. The line was very faint and I heard this pathetic little voice saying, 'Kath, send me some food out here.' I burst out laughing. Both he and Mike Hendrick were very ill with dysentery and were spending most of their time, like the old ladies of the song, 'locked in the lavatory'.

It happened that I had arranged to spend the weekend with Kath Hendrick. I must admit that we both found the situation highly amusing although we realized the seriousness behind the call for help. We spent Friday planning menus consisting of foodstuffs which could be consumed straight from the can requiring neither heating nor reconstituting with water. Saturday morning found us at Sainsbury's supermarket purchasing the same and Saturday afternoon finding out how to get it there. This was a situation where a 'name' came come in very handy. 'Botham? Pakistan? Are you any relation of . . . Oh, in that case, if we can put an article in the local paper we'll get it there for you free of charge.' They were very helpful and a few days later Ian rang in a much more cheerful frame of mind with a big thank-you from the whole team who had shared in the bounty.

Over the years there have been many stories about touring conditions; some sound unbelievable but most of them are true. In one of the guest houses, Ian shared a room with J. K. Lever and Roddy, a large, bewhiskered rat of whom they eventually became quite fond. Sometimes on tour all plans for a balanced team have to be abandoned and it becomes a case of, 'If you can stand up, you're in.' I should say at once that many of the international hotels in the larger towns are of a high standard and hold no fears for the intrepid traveller. Ian has always maintained that the people of Pakistan are the friendliest of hosts, but customs and climate are so different to ours there are great difficulties in adapting. I have often discussed this with other wives and we are all of the same opinion. If an England football team were there for several weeks, without doubt the authorities would ensure that satisfactory food and accommodation were available. I am fairly certain that the officials of the TCCB and their wives never find it necessary to cheer on the team in Pakistan, though they are there in force in Australia, New Zealand and certain of the West Indian islands. The BBC also seem to find it necessary to have a large workforce in Australia while managing with one lonely commentator in Pakistan and India.

It took Ian and Mike Hendrick in particular a while to recover from their illness, and most of the other players were ill to a lesser degree. When the plane left the runway en route to New Zealand a resounding cheer went up from all the members of the touring party.

6

Celebrity Beckons

'Hot shot Botham is England Star' – *Daily Express.*
'Botham is Tops' – *Sun.*
'Botham in Full Bloom' – *Daily Telegraph.*
'Botham Shines in Test Spectacular' – *Daily Mail.*

As can be seen from the above headlines, Ian had a very successful time in New Zealand. The highlight for his family was his maiden century in the second Test. All through the night, at two minutes past each hour, there used to be a Test match special score update. In those days my brain seemed to have a clock inside it and I would wake at exactly the right time to listen in to the voice of Don Mosey who, at that time, was a good friend of ours. At 2.02 a.m. Ian was 32 not out and going well. At 3.02 a.m. he was 74 not out and going even better. I didn't need my internal clock from then on because I could no longer sleep, and drank endless cups of hot chocolate as I paced the floor.

At 4.02 the newscaster took us to Christchurch, New Zealand. Ian had reached a maiden Test century. At a later date when discussing the event I realized why both our parents' phones were engaged at that time in the morning. We had all listened and simultaneously tried to contact each other.

Ian went on from strength to strength, making runs and taking wickets. The England team had been decimated by the advent of Mr Kerry Packer and his cricket 'circus', but the sportswriter Alex Bannister was to say in an article from New Zealand, 'Botham has made the loss of Tony Greig negligible and I think English cricket has found a player with all the gifts and charisma of Keith Miller.'

It is relevant to mention at this point one thing which always annoys me: so many people, many of whom should know better, state that the Packer exodus of England players gave Ian his place in the national side. In fact, he had played two Test matches and two one-day Internationals under the leadership of Tony Greig and alongside Bob Woolmer, Alan Knott and Derek Underwood, who later played for Packer. On several occasions I have actually pointed this out to sportswriters who have said, 'Oh yes. You're right,' and then proceeded to write the same old twaddle.

During the summer of 1978, Test matches were again played against Pakistan and New Zealand. Once again Ian did well throughout both series. I was just twenty-two and Ian twenty-one. I think it is natural that we both welcomed the publicity and were flattered by the constant attention paid to us by the press. I must admit that I revelled in Ian's success. By this time Ian had an agent, Reg Hayter, who always had our interests at heart. He became a confidant and family friend and, together with his wife Lucy, gave us all the support and help we needed.

Things were going well generally, sponsorship deals were being negotiated, newspapers were clamouring for exclusive articles and were prepared to pay for them, and Ian Botham was a person much in demand at cricket dinners, pro-am golf tournaments, benefit matches for other players, radio and television interviews all over the country. Ian travelled the length and breadth of England, meeting anyone he was asked to meet, playing wherever he was asked to play. For a while I accepted this graciously as a necessary ingredient of success, until I realized just what it was doing to our lives.

Until now we had been able to plan ahead with a reasonable assumption that whatever we planned would take place. Suddenly I realized that this wasn't happening any longer, other events were taking precedence and Liam and I were having to be fitted in around them, where possible.

Early in that season, as I was no longer working, we had decided to rent a house in Somerset in order to spend more time together as a family. This turned out to be an absolute failure. For fifty per cent of the county season the Somerset team were away from home and, as was the case in subsequent years, Ian was selected for every Test match. There were usually five, plus the 'one-days'. All Tests take place in London or Birmingham, equidistant from either Humberside or Somerset, and at Manchester, Nottingham and Leeds, all of which are practically on our northern doorstep. There I was in the West Country. In addition to my lonely winters I found myself enjoying a pretty lonely summer. Not wanting to take Ian's place in Test matches for granted, we repeated the experiment the following year, and found it equally unsuccessful.

In case anyone reading has the impression that I spent most of our early years together complaining, nothing is further from the truth. We had lots of good times together and lots of fun, though 'together' may not be the operative word. We rarely found ourselves in this happy state and when we did there were countless other people there too. Ian finds it difficult to say 'no'. It is admirable that he was determined that all his old friends should still be a part of his life. In addition to all the functions – mostly stag – which were being arranged for him, what little time Ian had left was usually spent on the golf courses of Somerset, popping into a favourite pub for a 'quick one' with his bachelor friends, or remaining behind at the end of a day's play to enjoy the social life at the county ground as had been his wont before I arrived to live there.

As many times as possible I went with him, but, even when the functions weren't officially 'stag', people seemed to forget that Ian was married and I just wasn't invited. When I was, I often felt very much like a spare part. In any case, having very little help with Liam, who was only nine months old when this season began, I quickly found that we really didn't fit into Ian's life at this time.

It wasn't altogether by amicable arrangement that I allowed this state of affairs to continue. It is true to say that we had more rows when I was living in Somerset than we had ever had before or since. I have seethed and raged on occasions too numerous to recall but, as anyone who has argued with Ian will know, he has a magical capacity to confuse an argument to such an extent that, in the end and against my will, I invariably found myself agreeing with him. Although never admitting his faults, these arguments generally led to me suddenly having a model husband for a day or two. He would arrange a baby-sitter and take me out for a meal, spend more time with Liam, and I would find myself able to put aside my slow cooker for a day or two, confident that Ian would be home on time to eat the under-done steak I had carefully prepared for him, just to his liking.

The one profound disagreement I do remember began over a trivial matter. We had rented a small house on a large estate for the summer and in the agreement was provision that we should care for the garden. One Sunday morning before a John Player League game Ian was having a 'lie in', a frequent occurrence in our early days. He had been promising for the last few days that, come Sunday, he would have a quick run round the lawn with the mower. When he eventually got up with just enough time left to do the lawn he suddenly remembered that he had to attend a meeting prior to the game. I saw red and the resulting argument had an unexpected ending. Intending to storm out of the house he masterfully went to open the door. Unfortunately this particular door occasionally stuck. It chose this moment to be awkward, so Ian tried to help it along with his foot. The catch held fast but the panel didn't and Ian's foot went straight through it. Trying to extricate himself he over-balanced and ended up on his back. At first I was dumbfounded, then I burst out laughing. This silenced Ian as he tried to muster his dignity before seeing the funny side of it. Between gales of laughter he did gather his wits sufficiently to say, 'There's no way I can cut the lawn now. I've just hurt my foot.' It didn't prevent him from playing cricket, though.

Cricket-wise, Ian had a fantastic summer. Newspapers waxed euphorical about his exploits in the Test arena: 'Bionic man Botham is a Test killer', 'Rip-roaring Ian', 'Botham Swings into History', are but a few of the headlines from that 1978 season.

Sitting at the Lord's Test match, having watched Ian take eight wickets in an innings and score a century – a world record for an all-round performance – I was trying to hedge questions about whether I would be joining Ian on the forthcoming winter tour of Australia. I had just begun to suspect that I might be pregnant again. If I was, then the new arrival would come about the first week in February and, on a tour starting at the beginning of November and ending in March, I didn't see how I could possibly make it to Australia. The TCCB actively discouraged wives from joining the tour during the first few weeks so when Ian's name was announced in the touring party again I had very mixed feelings. Both of us, having experienced the long separation of the previous tour, had vowed that we would never be parted for so long again.

Having consulted my obstetrician, I was pronounced fit enough to travel on condition that I was back under her care by the middle of December. If I wanted to have any time worth mentioning, it meant leaving home very shortly after Ian. The by-now-familiar contract came through the post. Note number 7 was headed 'Wives on Tour'. Wives would be welcome, it stated. A formal request to join husbands had to be put before the Board and we would be notified in due course whether permission had been given.

I wrote the letter, Ian signed it, and off it went. There was no formal reply but about four o'clock one afternoon there was a telephone call from Donald Carr to Ian who was out shooting on a neighbouring farm. He wouldn't tell me what it concerned, except that it related to my application to join Ian in Australia. Ian's return call began politely enough, with an explanation of exactly why I had to go so early. In fact, throughout that evening and throughout the many telephone calls from Mr Carr, who was obviously following instructions from the TCCB, Ian progressively became more and more frustrated but remained polite, if firm. Each negative response fuelled his determination that I should spend some time out there with him, until his patience snapped and, to my horror, I heard him say, 'Very well, Donald, if you won't allow my wife to join me I shall withdraw from the tour.'

Ian had a good night's sleep while I tossed and turned. An early telephone call the next day brought permission for me to go not earlier than ten days from their arrival in Australia and with the proviso that I must leave before the first Test match began. I think this left me with about two and a half weeks there. This was confirmed in writing and, for the moment, I accepted it. Heaven knows what would have happened had we not been prepared to compromise.

Looking back after nine tours, I don't think either of us would change our attitude today. We knew what was right for us. Ian is happier, and therefore plays better, in the knowledge that at some stage of the tour I shall be with him. I fully realize that a team travelling together for four to five months must build a special rapport and forge a bond; both on and off the pitch 'the team' is special. In all hotels a room is set aside for a 'team room', and this is rightly regarded as a sanctum where players can meet and let off steam and where team spirit can be cemented; thus it is a 'no-go' area for women. I would never have dreamed of putting pressure on Ian to break this bond. I wouldn't have managed it anyway! I know that most of the wives I have toured with feel the same. There is, as always in life, the odd exception where a player perhaps loses team identity with the arrival of a wife or girlfriend, but it is a very rare exception and I don't understand the anxiety of the 'powers that be' to control our decision whether or not to join our husbands for some part of the tour. It isn't as though we are given any help financially, nor do they accept responsibility for us.

As I write this I am sipping a glass of champagne to celebrate the grand slam of triumphs in Australia during the tour of 1986–87. I hear that never before has a team been so successful nor a touring side so happy. I know that to be true; I spent seven weeks out there with my family, along with almost all the other wives. We have never before been made so welcome. I rest my case.

The last Saturday at home prior to Ian's departure on the 1978–79 arrived and, with it, a surprise farewell party at the 'Queen's Head' in Epworth, the headquarters of Ian's Sunday League football team. I was busy, together with my mother and Julie from next door, shortening umpteen pairs of trousers and sewing in dozens of name-tapes while wondering how to get Ian to the party as he had just stated that there was a good film on television he wanted to watch. In the end I had to tell him there was a bit of a farewell party arranged and almost had to push him out of the door with my father.

A very short time later we heard the car being revved up outside the window and a lot of whispering and shushing. I looked through the window to see Ian propped against the wall with his hand held high above his head.

'What on earth is happening?' I asked.

'Nothing much,' said Dad. 'Ian's cut his hand on some glass which just needs a stitch. Absolutely no need to worry. I'm just taking him along to casualty. We'll be back soon.'

Shortly afterwards a group of friends arrived to tell us what had happened. Two of them were obviously very shaken as they had unwittingly caused this freak accident.

Ian had left a group in the main bar to go through to the pool room. Just as he was about to follow someone through the swing door, another friend shouted his name. Ian turned his head and at the same time put out his hand to prevent the door closing on him. There were four panels of glass in the upper part and it was on a sprung hinge that allowed it to swing both ways. His hand went straight through the glass and in an instinctive reaction he pulled it quickly back towards him, severing two tendons and coming within a hair's breadth of also severing a nerve.

We didn't know the extent of the damage until the following day. Ian arrived home in the early hours of the morning with his hand and arm heavily swathed in bandages. 'I've to go back in the morning,' he said. 'It's nothing much, but they brought a specialist out and he wants to take a look under anaesthetic just to make sure that there're no slivers of glass left in the wound.' I didn't believe him. I knew it was worse than he said, but no amount of probing would get him to say any more. He wouldn't allow me to go with him to hospital the next morning: 'Your father will take me. I don't want you hanging about in hospitals. There's no need for it. Don't worry.' As if I could stop worrying when I knew as well as he did that his whole career was now hanging in the balance.

We rang Donald Carr and informed him of the accident. His instructions were to say nothing to anyone. They, the TCCB would deal with everything.

The long day passed and I went to see Ian in the evening when he had recovered from the anaesthetic. While I was there the specialist, Mr Kahn, came in to see him with reassuring words: 'There has been a severing of the tendons but fortunately no damage to the nerve. It will take about three weeks to heal but there should be a complete recovery with no permanent damage.'

Everyone we knew in Epworth came to visit that evening inquiring anxiously how Ian was faring. The lads who had organized the party were devastated, assuming a responsibility which wasn't theirs for what had happened. 'You mustn't blame yourselves,' I kept repeating. 'You should know by now that Ian is always the one if accidents occur.'

Donald Carr had asked for a report from the specialist treating Ian who had advised that he should continue with the tour as planned, convinced that by the time the first Test match began the arm would have healed.

Later that evening my mother, who was staying with me while Ian was still in hospital, and I settled down to relax after a hectic day when there was a loud knock on the door. Ten o'clock, late callers! It was a reporter from one of the national dailies. 'Good evening,' he said. 'Mrs Botham? We've had a report that your husband has been badly injured in a pub brawl and is unlikely to be able to go on tour. Would you confirm that?'

'I've nothing to say,' I replied, firmly abiding by the instructions of the TCCB.

'Oh, come on, I've already got the story and if you say nothing we'll print it anyway. I've been sent all the way from Manchester for this.'

I really don't remember his words following this, but I remember him getting quite abusive and very angry when I refused to say anything. Nor would he leave my house into which, out of politeness, I had at first invited him. We stood in the kitchen. It was my first personal introduction to the less attractive side of the press. 'Well,' he said finally, 'I'll go now but I'll find someone who *will* tell me about it.'

He went to the pub nearby and cross-questioned Bill the landlord about every detail of our life. He even asked how much we had paid for our house. Exasperated, Bill eventually asked him to leave. From there he trailed around Epworth questioning everyone he met, going from hostelry to hostelry until he finally arrived at the right one. There, as always, ranks were closed and he could get no one to disclose anything except the basic facts. The people of Epworth learned early how to deal with reporters: you say nothing and refuse to be goaded into making remarks which can be twisted or taken more than one way.

An SOS to Dad brought him over to deal with any further unwanted visitors. He found the reporter actually in the act of phoning his headquarters, hearing him say, 'You can kill that story about Botham, there's nothing in it.' However, a story did appear the next day with enough innuendos to grey, if not blacken, Ian's name.

Ian travelled to Australia with the rest of the team. As predicted his arm healed with no ill effects – Mr Kahn and the Doncaster Royal Infirmary had done a marvellous job – and I arrived for my brief visit.

I took young Liam, who was fifteen months old, with

me, and I was six-and-a-half months pregnant. The other wives had not, of course, arrived so early in the tour, and Ian was heavily committed to cricket during the day. Not, you may think, an ideal situation in which to visit a strange country. I didn't regret my decision to go one little bit. I liked Australia from the moment I arrived, finding everyone I met helpful and kind, eager to show off their lovely country. This time I visited Brisbane, Sydney and Melbourne. As always there was much to see but I refrained from rushing about too much, spending most of my time enjoying the hot sunshine, lazing by the pool or on the beaches with Liam. Now that Ian is joining Queensland for three seasons I have been asked many times whether we would consider emigrating to Australia. The answer has to be 'no', because we all love England too much and because our families are here, but we count ourselves fortunate to be able to visit Australia so frequently and hope to continue to do so.

On that first tour I kept so much in the background that the manager, Doug Insole, entering the lift after me one morning said, 'Oh, I'd heard you'd arrived but I've not seen you about.' I told him that because of all the fuss prior to Ian's departure I had deliberately kept a low profile, not knowing how I would be received by the hierarchy. They were, he said, 'Delighted to have me along' and went on to say that he was surprised to hear that I wasn't staying for the first Test!

I had been home from Australia a matter of hours when I was contacted by the BBC sports department. The voting had been taking place for the BBC Sports Personality of the Year and I was told that Ian was very much in the running to win it. Would I be prepared to travel to London? they asked. The prizes were being presented by Prince Charles and it would be nice for me to be there if Ian won. I wasn't too keen on travelling to London just then; I had just come off a long-haul flight and was still somewhat jet-lagged. My second baby was due in about six weeks and Liam, at sixteen months, was still turning night into day after his return from down-under.

However, I decided it would be churlish to refuse. Liam was left with good old Mum (no doubt to sleep until midnight and then get up and want to play), while Dad drove me to London. In those days I had no nanny, and it was difficult to drop everything and shoot off at a moment's notice.

Arriving at Shepherd's Bush I was greeted by Cliff Morgan, head of BBC sport. He was very welcoming. At the time I knew virtually nobody in sport except cricketers and was then very reticent about making myself known in strange company.

Cliff obviously had many people to speak to, so he took me along to the entertainment room and someone introduced me to the wife of another sporting celebrity. She didn't stop talking for a minute, all about people I had never even heard of, and she was extremely boring. No one else came anywhere near us and I had the distinct impression that we had been paired off because no one quite knew what to do with us. As I looked around the room I could see that everyone else was a celebrity of some sort in their own right. I began to wish I hadn't come, then I saw someone I recognized as an international sportswoman, someone, in fact, with whom Ian and I had spent time in Australia in company with others. As she passed by me I spoke to her, 'Oh,' she said pausing for a moment, 'nice to see you again. Excuse me,' and walked away. Obviously Ian and Kathryn Botham together were far more interesting to her than Kathryn Botham alone. I wish she hadn't made it quite so obvious.

I retired to a corner with my drink, contemplating the crowd around me. Many of them smiled if they caught my eye and, I'm sure, were extremely interesting and pleasant people but at that time I didn't have that 'ring of confidence' that would allow me to risk another snub. I was relieved when Prince Charles arrived. A chosen few, who did not include me, were presented to him and we were informed that the show was about to start.

I walked tight-lipped down the corridor clutching my official pass and turned at a door marked 'Audience'. 'No, Mrs Botham,' said the doorman, 'that's a participant's ticket.'

Participant! I panicked. I had no idea that I had been asked along to participate. It had already been made clear to me that, should Ian win, the trophy would be awarded to him in Australia, so I wasn't there for that. What then?

I took my seat in a daze. Technicians hurried everywhere. I had been placed near a group of footballers. I forget their names but they were very friendly. Then an official appeared and proceeded to fasten a microphone to my dress. 'What's this for?' I asked. 'Oh, Frank Bough is going to have a word or two with you during the programme,' I was told. I demurred, so Frank came along for a word there and then. 'Don't worry,' he said, 'I'm just going to ask you a couple of questions like, how old is your little boy and what are you doing this Christmas.'

I don't remember anything about the beginning of the programme. Had I known what they wanted, I would never have gone. I didn't like publicity then, and I'm still not too happy about it, although now I think I cope with it better.

When Ian was introduced he appeared on a huge screen and Frank Bough, after chatting with him for a few moments, said, 'I have a surprise for you, Ian, your wife Kathryn is here with us this evening.' Then turning to me he said, 'Now, Kathy, what have you to say to each other?'

We had lots to say but not in front of millions of people.

I am told I carried the situation off pretty well – I wouldn't know whether I did or not. I remember the evening as an ordeal, and Ian didn't win either! I think it taught me a lot, though. I have learned to ask very carefully what is expected of me before accepting an engagement, then I can prepare appropriately. It also helped me greatly in my attitude towards the life I was beginning to lead. I remembered how lost and ill-equipped I felt in such a star-studded environment and the anger I felt when I seemed to be ignored. I have come a long way from those early days when I sat in my corner with my drink thinking, 'I can't talk to Gareth Edwards about rugby or Alex Higgins about snooker and I certainly can't bore them with tales about me or a discussion on the weather.'

One of the many bonuses of being married to Ian is that I am in a position to meet celebrities from many walks of life. I take great pleasure in this and find most of them interesting, thoughtful and kind – the others you can steer clear of. I now know that when I chat to Eric Clapton, Elton John, or Denis Lilley they don't particularly want to talk about music or cricket, they want to talk family or the world news or listen to a joke. Neither Ian nor I seek friendships with celebrities. Our friendships have all grown naturally and our true friends all mean a great deal to us whether they are in or out of the public eye.

Looking back to those early times when I was so unsure of how to approach 'personalities' I began to realize how many of our friends must have felt in those days of approaching fame. When Ian was away they were fantastic. I was included in their plans, and never allowed to feel odd man out. When he returned they would need reassuring that they should still come. They seemed to be in awe, and a good friend once said, 'I really don't know what to say to him.' At first I laughed and replied 'Oh, he's quite normal really,' but then, perhaps for the first time, realized how hard you have to work at true friendship. At our frequent parties the guest list always starts with all our friends from the early days and added to it are the names of those who have given us friendship, support and loyalty through the years. How dare a newspaper critic commenting on the recent 'Forty Minutes' television programme talk about 'Botham's hangers-on'! We know better than to invite hangers-on into our home.

Living so much of our lives apart, I found myself in the position of creating alone the ties between neighbours and others I would meet in the normal course of events. Then Ian would be home for a while. Amazingly he is shy of meeting new people. Those close to him recognize this in him but it is a difficulty I had to overcome when introducing him to new friends I had made in his absence. I often had quite a job to persuade him to accept invitations. In almost every instance he would begin a new acquaintance by being guarded, then would relax and quickly become the life and soul of the party. In the same way I suppose you could say I was guarded when I met the friends Ian made as he journeyed around the world.

I don't find it at all difficult to settle down to a normal family life at home – cooking, shopping, meeting the children from school, watching Liam play for his school rugby or cricket team or Sarah in her Brownie play or taking her pony riding. I enjoy my life in this context but I also enjoy my 'other life' and count myself fortunate in having both. When I leave my home behind me and speed towards London or wherever, I step into what is, to me, another world among different people, many of whom are household names. I am able to enjoy the 'perks' of being Ian's wife and life becomes easier.

What I do find difficult is marrying the two lives together. I can only do this in the company of people I know well.

During that winter of 1978–79 after my return from Australia I once again awaited the arrival of a new baby. The bad winter had put a stop to building alterations on our house; no central heating and a tarpaulin for a kitchen ceiling was not too good in the depth of winter, plus the fact that forecasters were predicting severe winter weather. One Sunday afternoon in late January snow began to fall, thickly and persistently. I remember giving Liam his tea in the kitchen, feeling uneasy about the fact that the snow was becoming deep and my house was eighteen miles away from the hospital along country roads.

A telephone call from Mum suggested that I should pack my bags and Dad would come over in the Land-Rover to pick up Liam and myself to stay with them as their house was much nearer the hospital and on main roads. I waited a long time for Dad and was becoming anxious when he arrived, explaining that he had stopped several times to pull people out of drifts. Epworth was cut off completely for four days.

The following Friday I went into hospital and on the Saturday Sarah Lianne arrived. Ian knew the arrival was imminent and, in fact, there was a phone call from Australia within five minutes of Sarah's birth. He was thrilled to be told he had a daughter; we both were. He amused the staff greatly by ringing up at every opportunity and I seemed to spend a great deal of my forty-eight hours in the maternity wing in a wheelchair being pushed at great speed towards the Sister's office to talk to Australia.

Sarah was two weeks old when Ian arrived home. Dad had gone down to London to meet him. I remember the door opening and Ian came in; he greeted us all, then said to Liam, 'Are you going to take Daddy to see your new sister?' They sat together on the end of the bed as Ian cradled his new daughter in his arms.

7

Captain's Wife

'The hottest property in Test cricket' is how one paper described Ian at the beginning of the 1979 season. He was in demand everywhere for television and radio shows, newspaper articles, speaking at dinners, opening sports halls, garages, bazaars, anything and everything. If he had accepted a quarter of what was asked he wouldn't have had time even to pick up a cricket bat. From this point life assumed such a frantic pace that I was left gasping for breath.

Trying to cope with a nineteen-month-old toddler, who was already beginning to follow in father's footsteps, a two-month-old baby and a very demanding husband was difficult to say the least, but by now I had learned to live with the reality which was that the children and I just had to fit into Ian's life where and when we could. Because Ian spent so little time with the children, he was unable to appreciate the limitations they impose upon one. He wanted us to go everywhere with him but then, of course, he would never be available to help with a mischievous toddler, a call of nature or a hungry baby. I wanted us to be a family together as much as possible, but I realized, if Ian didn't, that just trying to be together was becoming impossible.

Wherever we went the demands on Ian's time were too

great. We would go to a cricket benefit match, for example, which has a very relaxed atmosphere; just the place, you would think, for a happy family day. We would set off, and upon arrival at the ground the car would immediately be swamped by autograph-hunters. Ian would head for the dressing-room as quickly as possible and ask Pete McCombe, a close friend, to come over and help with pushchairs, travelling rugs and the hundred and one things you need for small children. I would find a spot to sit, preferably away from earnest-looking cricketing gentlemen who could be guaranteed to find the presence of children annoying. Then the day would progress, not smoothly, but in fits and starts: 'Mummy, wee wee', 'Ice-cream', 'See Daddy.' If I took my eyes off Liam to attend to Sarah he would attempt to do a disappearing trick or to join Daddy on the field of play. I used to breathe a sigh of relief when Annie Denning appeared with daughters Claire and Sammy.

Thankfully, Sarah was a good baby and posed problems only at feeding times – the problem being the lack of facilities for feeding and changing babies. I usually resorted to the car, to the great interest of that band of spectators who apparently gain pleasure from wandering through the carpark looking at cricketers' cars. The end of play brought no relief as we rarely got away quickly, there was always so much for Ian to do. It took him ages to shower and change and then I would hear, 'I just want Ian to meet – you don't mind do you, Mrs Botham?' or Ian would say, 'I promised to have a quick drink with – , I haven't seen him for ages.' By this time Liam and Sarah would normally have been tucked up in bed and, as all mums know, an over-tired toddler can become impossible. I was very conscious of being looked at disapprovingly, obviously I was thought to be an irresponsible young mother by some of the mature ladies, though it was probably their husbands who were delaying Ian!

In contrast to this, Ian would probably have spent his day partly on the field of play, then sitting in the dressing-room with a cup of tea, chatting to friends, reading the newspaper, playing cards and generally having a sociable time. In the early days of benefit matches he would come and sit with me when not actually participating in the game, but now this was impossible because of the flood of autograph-hunters every time he made an appearance. Now and then he would ask someone to pop out to see if I was OK. I always said 'Yes' simply because there was no point in saying 'No'.

Frequently on the car journey home he would turn to me and say, 'Had a good day?' 'Mmm,' I would more often than not reply, 'I could have done with leaving earlier, though.' As always he would have a perfectly reasoned and well-thought-out excuse which I couldn't fault, but looking at our two sleeping children I would sometimes wonder why I took such pains to further the bond between the three of them. Ian had achieved fame and was obviously enjoying it. If it left little or no time to spend with us then he seemed to accept it. In the Test team at that time, apart from Derek Randall, who was not consistently selected, he seemed to be the only one with young children which didn't help either Ian or myself. In times of frustration I would actually say, 'We should never have had them.' Ian would become angry at this and say, 'But I'm doing all this for you, Liam and Sarah.'

I seem to be repeating myself when I say Ian had a good season that year but that was the way it went. Wickets, runs and catches came in abundance. During the second Test match at Lord's against India he took his 100th Test wicket in the shortest time ever. I was there that day with all the family plus parents, parents-in-law, my sister Lindsay and her fiancé Paul. Lindsay must have foreseen this event, for she solved the problem of getting enough tickets for us all by winning a prize in the *Sunday Telegraph* 'Cricketer of the Year' competition. She had to answer eight questions on cricket, nominate her cricketer of the year and write a slogan in not more than ten words giving the reason for her choice. Ian was her choice and her catchphrase was, 'Consistently amazing and amazingly consistent.' Her prize was two tickets for the Lord's Test match.

Between us we looked after Liam, taking it in turns to amuse him with walks around the ground. We should have taken bets as to which one of us wouldn't see Ian take his wicket. As it happens, it was me! As for Sarah, the Metropolitan police force make very good babysitters. They were kind enough to watch over her while she slept peacefully in her pram at the back of the stand.

Shortly afterwards Ian achieved the double of one thousand runs and one hundred wickets in record time, after only twenty-one Test matches. He was pleased to receive, among others, a congratulatory telegram from the daughter of Vinoo Mankad, the previous record-holder who had achieved this in twenty-three Test matches for India back in the early 1950s.

When the touring party for Australia was announced at the end of the season it was no surprise to learn that Ian was in the squad. This time there were no problems to threaten me joining them at some stage. I chose to have Christmas at home and fly out for the final stages of the tour.

Early in the tour it was announced that Ian had been appointed as a tour selector and the press was rife with speculation that he might be in line for selection as captain the following summer. It was also by now becoming apparent that everyone was beginning to expect the impossible, that Ian should score centuries and take five wickets in every innings. Two or three wickets and 49 runs were classed as failures as he was expected to be the leading wicket-taker and highest run-scorer in every match.

Only three Test matches were played in Australia as England were going on to Bombay to play in the Jubilee Test match. I chose not to go with the children to India and instead visited Pete and Annie Denning who were spending the winter in Perth.

I had forgotten all about the Jubilee match when I rang home to make inquiries as to the progress of the purchase of our new house in Epworth. A few days before Ian had left for the tour he had announced we were moving round the corner into a bigger house he had noticed was up for sale. As usual he had made the decision and I was left to sort out the minor details – like the price, finding an agent, selling our existing house, bargaining, etcetera.

We had almost settled before I left for Australia and we were to exchange contracts immediately on our return. I rang home to check that everything was going smoothly. Mum answered the phone, obviously slightly irritated, and greeted me with, 'Aren't you listening to the cricket from Bombay? Ian is just about to break another record.' We didn't have the chance to hear it in Perth, so from Australia I listened to the radio in England via the telephone and heard that Ian had scored a century and taken ten wickets in the same match – in fact he took thirteen wickets altogether. This Test record still stands. Bob Taylor also broke a record by becoming the first wicket-keeper to claim ten victims in the same match.

Ian was everybody's hero except mine. I caught the Qantas flight out of Perth which was being joined by the team at Bombay. Having changed my first-class ticket to travel tourist so that I could sit with Ian, I was not charmed to have him fall asleep immediately on take-off to wake again at Heathrow.

Speculation regarding the captaincy of England was growing as Mike Brearley confirmed he had made his last tour but wouldn't confirm whether or not he would accept the captaincy at home against the West Indies. In a poll conducted for BBC 2's 'Newsnight', eight out of fifteen county captains chose Ian as a successor to Brearley.

I knew that Ian very much wanted the captaincy and I was naive enough, at that time, to want it for him. Everything seemed to have gone well so far in his career and there was no reason to suppose that they wouldn't continue to do so. Therefore it was a cause for celebration when he rang to say that he had been offered the captaincy of England. Another honour came his way about this time: he was extremely proud to be made Epworth's first Honorary Townsman.

I made up my mind now that I was not prepared to go through another summer of running myself ragged between my husband who wanted me with him and my children who needed me at home. Thus it was that Diane entered our lives. She came initially as a nanny for the summer months between leaving college and beginning full-scale nursing training. Seven years later she is still with us, very much part of the family.

Contrary to what people might expect, I did not leave the children behind. It was just that nanny came too, ever mindful of our desire to keep the family together as much as possible. Having Diane meant that I could join in with things much more easily. After matches I could join Ian for a drink and a chat with friends instead of joining the children at their bathtime. Ian could accept for both of us rather than have to accept for himself and make excuses for me. There were so many things he just had to attend.

Now we could both go, secure in the knowledge that back at the hotel the children were well cared for.

At home I also had a freedom I had not known before. It was great to say, 'Yes, I can be there in an hour or so', when Ian rang to say, 'Meet me at Birmingham', or Leicester, or wherever, as he was wont to do.

Ian had been appointed captain for the two one-day Internationals against the West Indies in that summer of 1980. England lost the first at Headingley by 24 runs and won the second at Lord's by three wickets. 'It's Captain Fantastic', 'Botham Rules', 'Captain Marvel', 'Incredible Hulk', 'Botham Leads England to Revenge'. I remember jumping up and down in the Q Stand at Lord's absolutely elated as Ian scored the winning runs to give England victory against all predictions. He had already been told of his appointment to lead England in the Test series against the West Indies.

England lost the first Test match very narrowly. Ian was depressed after coming so close to winning. The second Test was drawn, as were all the others, so England went down in the series, one-nil. Perhaps if the England team had held on to their catches and won the first Test match things would have worked out very differently. A winning captain is always a good one, a losing captain soon disenchants the press, and we quickly discovered that now Ian could do nothing right. Perhaps in the same way that success breeds success, failure breeds failure and he was not able to produce the same performances as captain that he had done for other skippers.

I have often been asked whether I felt that the captaincy affected his play. I would hear Ian refuting this and wonder. At that time I read the papers and they seemed to contain a constant barrage of criticism. I noticed that the bonhomie of the majority of the press appeared to be evaporating when we met them. This may have been partly my fault as I was angry at their continuing verbal assaults: they had campaigned for him to be made captain and now the very same people were saying what a mistake the selectors had made. I have never learned to throw off the taunts of the press and have also never learned to hide my feelings. I couldn't bring myself to smile and talk with men who had just filed copy slating the very person with whom they were now wanting to mix socially. We didn't allow the situation to get us down too much and actually had some very good times. We helped each other through the bad times and being able to spend so much of the summer together was a bonus. We were invited into the royal box at Wimbledon and went to see *The King and I* where we met Yul Brynner, someone I had always wanted to meet. I wasn't disappointed.

Back at home, though, when out shopping I began to feel personally responsible for England's poor performance. I was taken to task by the butcher, the baker and everyone else. Everybody was ready to offer advice as to how Ian should tackle the job and quick to make such consoling remarks as, 'He's not doing very well, is he?' 'About time he got a few wickets.'

One weekend in Somerset I was walking round the ground with Marie, discussing the problems, when I heard a sharp voice say 'Mrs Botham?' 'Yes,' we both replied. Looking at me the owner of the voice said, 'You're Ian's wife, aren't you? You ought to tell that husband of yours that he is a disgrace to the side.' He carried on with his verbal abuse but I was so taken aback I didn't hear any more. I wondered then what satisfaction it gave him to have a go at me. Nor could I understand the nasty letters I received, addressed to me but vilifying Ian. Some were so bad and threatening that in the end we decided to pass them on to the police. Over the years Ian's life has been threatened several times and on one occasion at Old

Trafford he played just having received a letter addressed to him at the ground, informing him that his life was forfeit. When this was followed by a similar message the next day, this time cut from newspaper print, the police were called in and, unknown to me at the time, I was watched by plainclothes policemen wherever I went. Ian must have felt himself to be a very vunerable target in the middle of that vast Test arena.

The selectors kept faith with Ian and appointed him as captain for the 1980–81 winter tour of the West Indies. I wasn't sure whether I was pleased or not; however, we could look forward to almost four months together as the tour didn't leave until mid-January.

Since living in Epworth, which is seven miles from Scunthorpe, Ian had become a keen follower of Scunthorpe United Football Club and, after first being invited to meet the players, he was invited to join them for training. Consequently, whenever he had free time during the season he would attend the morning training sessions and invariably return home with colleagues for a game of snooker. Diane and I became dab hands at producing corned beef and Branston pickle sandwiches and mugs of tea – even at times having to ring wives to say their husbands had been 'unavoidably delayed'. The first time he was picked to play in Scunthorpe Reserves team he was almost as thrilled as when he was chosen to play cricket for England. I have spent many winter evenings on the wooden benches in the main stand at Scunthorpe cheering on the reserve team.

Away from the sporting arena and the usual preparations for the tour, I took delight in the novelty of having my partner with me at social gatherings in our home area plus the freedom from cricket and all the hassle that had accompanied it during the previous months.

It was going to be Ian's first Christmas at home with the

children and so during our annual autumn holiday in
Scotland I managed to prise him away from his salmon
fishing for half a day to go shopping in Glasgow. What a
good time we had choosing for Liam and Sarah – Tonka
toys, dolls and lots of stocking-fillers.

My sister Lindsay was married immediately after this
holiday and she and her husband Paul had planned to
come home for Christmas so that we could all be together.
Marie and Les were having Christmas at home as Wendy,
Ian's younger sister, had also recently married but they
planned to come north to spend the New Year with us.
For the second time in our married lives we were in the
throes of planning what was to us a very important family
time.

We were invited to several Christmas parties which we
looked forward to attending, but there was one party to
which I was not invited: the Scunthorpe United players'
Christmas 'do' – in other words a night on the town!

I was not at all keen on this and tried tactfully to suggest
to Ian that he shouldn't go. He was adamant that he
should. At that time Ian was a member of the Scunthorpe
playing staff and, true to form, if the staff were having a
get-together then he must be there. 'What would the lads
think, if I didn't go? I'm part of the club. I train with
them. I can't refuse to socialize with them.'

Ian was fighting to remain true to his conviction that
nothing must change. Stardom mustn't be allowed to alter
friendships or a way of life. Nobody would ever accuse
him of an 'off with the old and on with the new' philosophy. To his credit many people have said of him that he
didn't let fame go to his head and that he remains the same
person he always has been. I could see, though, that he
was finding it difficult to come to terms with the restrictions that being in the limelight inevitably brings in its
wake.

I found myself in a tricky situation. Reg Hayter, Ian's agent, had been suggesting to me for some time that I should try and wean Ian away from his football. The TCCB weren't too keen on it and this total commitment of his to Scunthorpe was beginning to become obsessional. Hint though I did that there were more important things than a team party and how uneasy I felt about it, he remained convinced that he must go.

Returning from this in the early hours of the morning he woke me up. I heard that it had gone off well but there had been a bit of trouble at the end as they were walking back to the minibus. A fellow had hurled abuse at Ian at the top of his voice in some extremely colourful language. Joe Neenan, the Scunthorpe goalkeeper, had tried to shut him up and a scuffle had ensued. I was alarmed to hear this and asked Ian straight away if he had allowed himself to become involved. 'Give me some credit,' was the reply, 'of course I didn't.' Satisfied, I turned over and went to sleep thinking no more about it.

The Saturday before Christmas I was preparing the children's tea when the front doorbell rang. I shouted to Ian to keep an eye on the children. I answered the door to two gentlemen who asked to see Ian. I thought they were press but they turned out to be plainclothes policemen who wished to talk to Ian regarding an incident which had taken place in Scunthorpe two days earlier. I felt sick and took them in to see Ian. Carrying on with the children's tea was a nightmare but for their sakes I tried to keep calm. Very shortly Ian came in to ask for the clothes he had worn that night. The shirt of course had been washed and ironed but the trousers had been hung up in the wardrobe.

'What on earth is going on?' I asked.

'Oh, nothing,' he said. 'Don't worry.'

The police left almost immediately, clutching a pair of shoes and his trousers. I was in a daze, it was the first time

I had ever had any dealings with the police other than in an advisory capacity when I needed to know the way or whether I was parking in the right spot. I am one of those people whose blood runs cold if a police car follows me when I'm driving. Ian repeated what he had said the previous evening but also told me that the lad concerned had claimed that Ian had beaten him up, and that he could produce witnesses. I was absolutely stunned and said that I couldn't believe it was happening. Ian sat me down and reasoned with me.

'Look, Kathryn,' he said, 'there really is nothing to worry about. I'll tell you exactly what happened. We came out of the nightclub – Joe and I were last because I had been delayed to sign lots of autographs. The other players had already disappeared to the minibus and as we walked after them this bastard hurled the most vile abuse after me. We ignored it for a while but he was yelling it across the street and using my name frequently, so I turned and told him to shut up. He just sneered and continued to walk after us still ranting and raving. Joe turned on him and he ran. Unfortunately, Joe ran after him. I stood for a while but was worried when I saw Joe disappear round a corner. I then ran myself to find Joe walking back towards me and the bastard was on the ground picking himself up. I just wanted to make sure he was all right so I helped him to his feet and told him that perhaps he wouldn't be so bloody stupid next time. As Joe and I walked back to the bus two more idiots appeared and shouted after us "We'll get you for this, Botham." Honest, Kath, that's it – don't worry about it, it's not going to spoil my Christmas.'

We decided not to let anyone know about it, so somehow we got through Christmas.

Between Christmas and New Year a telephone call from Pat Gibson of the *Daily Express* warned us that the press had got hold of the story. I believe that the person concerned, a sailor by the name of Steven Isbister, had been in touch with the *Express*. I do know that Pat Gibson met him at the 'Jolly Sailor' at Gunness near his home.

We rang Alan Herd, our solicitor, immediately. With hindsight we should have rung him straight after the incident had occurred. We now had to inform the family, as we knew they would be inundated with press calls. The papers had a field day inferring that this weak little sailor, serving in Her Majesty's Navy, had been bullied and beaten by none other than the England cricket captain. I hardly remember Joe's name being mentioned. I do remember, though, how devastated Joe was. He came round to see us and told me that he couldn't understand the fuss. 'I did hit him,' he said, 'he bloody well deserved it, but I've told everyone so. Ian had nothing to do with it, what are they getting at him for?'

When the press revealed the name of this poor little six-foot sailor we had several offers of help. It was made clear to us that he was a known trouble-maker. He and his friends had terrorized a local elderly fish-and-chip shop owner and had been bound over for a breach of the peace.

At the time, though, this didn't help us. A Scottish MP wrote a very sanctimonious article in a daily newspaper saying in effect that just because Ian Botham was England's cricket captain he should not be allowed to escape justice. Where is the justice in being prejudged by people who didn't know any of the background and before we even knew ourselves whether the case was to go to court? Joe had already admitted his guilt at a magistrates' court and stated publicly that the blame was entirely his and that Ian had been in no way concerned. The article seemed to clinch the decision and we were informed that Ian was to be prosecuted. 'Let the courts decide' was the phrase used by the chief constable.

Both the police and the press, who must – like us – have

known of Isbister's record, chose to take none of it into consideration. Before Ian's appearance at Grimsby Crown Court (by his choice) later that year, he was made out to be very much the villain and Isbister very much the wronged hero. It also transpired at the court hearing that two of Isbister's so-called witnesses to the incident had a significant number of convictions for criminal offences, although neither of them would have been much over the age of twenty at the time in question – all of which was pointed out to the police by our lawyers before the decision to prosecute was taken. Yet despite this, Ian, myself and our family had to go through the indignity and circus spectacle of a trial based on allegations by such people. I still, to this day, think the whole affair was outrageous and would never have happened if Ian Botham had been 'Fred Smith'.

The TCCB stood by Ian on this occasion and amid all the speculation as to whether the England captaincy should be given to someone else, they reminded everyone that under our law a man is innocent until proven guilty. Therefore they would do nothing until the result of the court case was known.

Because of Ian's commitments, Alan Herd had asked that the case should be deferred and the police had offered no objection. So knowing that this case would not be resolved until the following September, I wondered, at times, how I could possibly survive until then. As information as to the progress of the defence filtered through to me I felt in turn elated and depressed. Like a Kelly doll I would bounce up only to find myself knocked flat again by an unhelpful comment.

The press coverage in the previous few months of Ian's so-called 'weight problem' faded into insignificance against this latest trauma – but the 'weight problem' had been bad enough at the time. An unguarded remark by the chairman

of the Test selectors, Alec Bedser, about Ian's apparent
weight gain had brought an almost hysterical wave of
publicity as to whether Ian had gained a few pounds or
not. Papers were full of 'before' and 'after' pictures. Diets
for cricketers were formulated and printed. All the shops,
pubs, hotels and fast-food shops in our area were visited
by journalists taking eager notes of where I shopped,
bribing shopkeepers to tell them whether we ate chips and
how big my grocery bill was. Neighbours were asked
whether they ever entertained us to meals and, if so, what
and how much did we eat. Liam, returning from nursery
school one day, was asked, 'What does Daddy eat for
breakfast?'

A young reporter from the *Daily Mail* camped outside
the house in his car for three days, appearing at the front
door every few hours to appeal for a story. At about the
tenth attempt he said to Mum, who was doing a sterling
job of keeping them all at bay, 'I know I'm being a bloody
nuisance. I keep ringing my editor to tell him there's no
chance but he just says I've got to get a story. Can I ask
you, does your daughter carry any excess weight?' At this
Mum just shouted, 'Kathryn, come here.' I'm five feet six
inches and weigh just eight stones. He looked at me and
remarked that I certainly didn't seem to over-eat. I gave
him some quotes after this and he went away relieved,
writing in fact quite a sympathetic article.

Ian has never been allowed to forget Mr Bedser's
remark, 'He's possibly carrying a pound or two too much.
If he is, he knows what to do.' Even to this day strangers
will come up to us in restaurants and say jokingly, but
irritatingly, 'You shouldn't eat that, you'll put on weight.'
At the time it was happening we couldn't go anywhere
without someone taunting him. People even shouted after
him in the street. I believe also that this had some bearing
on the Isbister affair at Scunthorpe, as no doubt some of

the abuse hurled at Ian would have concerned his weight.

Add to these disastrous events the fact that Ian was due to go off to the West Indies very shortly, and the result was one very dejected wife. I really didn't know how I could bear it. Somehow I did. Though our skies were very heavily clouded and at times we looked in vain for the silver lining, as day followed day things began to look a little less black.

Ian set off for the tour as usual, able to push the unwanted thoughts to the back of his mind. I knew the matches against the West Indies would be hard and the tour was being threatened by politicians in Guyana who objected to some South African connections on the part of certain of the England players. Some key players had opted not to tour or were injured, and Ian was thus leading a weakened team, but when he rang, as he frequently did, he sounded cheerful and this helped me. I knew he was worried about me; he had had to leave me to cope with all the fuss and once again I became the link-man between him and Alan Herd.

When things go wrong, they certainly seem to go wrong with a vengeance, but I thought they could only get better and as long as I held fast to this philosophy I managed to keep going.

8

Trials and Tribulations

Once Ian had actually gone, my fears about the next few months began to retreat. The pressures began to lift, the constant barrage of telephone calls slackened off and our home ceased to resemble a busy bed-and-breakfast place. My only immediate problem was persuading Liam that he really did like play-school.

Perversely, I didn't really enjoy my new-found peace. My life with Ian has a very definite two-tier system: I never have a minute to spare, rushing from one engagement to another, having a home full of friends, or talking on the telephone for what seems hours; even during our rare spells alone we seem to spend the time discussing how much we can fit in to our short spells together. Then he is gone, and with him the excitement. Life becomes flat and dull for a while until I readjust to life without him.

The side for the West Indies tour contained a good proportion of young players appearing for the first time. Looking through the names I realized that I knew very few of the wives and, as they came from all parts of the country, it was unlikely that they would know each other. Most of them were going to Barbados and I thought it might be a good idea if we all got to know each other in advance.

I set to work and thoroughly enjoyed organizing a

weekend party for as many as were able to attend. I arranged open house from Friday till Sunday. Apart from Brenda Gooch, who already had a family commitment, I was delighted that they all came and we had a really enjoyable get-together. I believe it was the first time a captain's wife had arranged anything like this and, as far as I know, there hasn't been anything similar since.

It worked very well. In the West Indies we greeted each other as old friends, having already met in a relaxed atmosphere, swopped stories and told of the joys, or otherwise, of England selection. I'm sure it helped us to know and understand not only each other but each other's husbands as well.

Shortly after this party I found myself acting as mentor to Gail, David Bairstow's wife. Her sister had told her of a report that the team were having a great time attending parties where women were flocking around them. Gail was very distressed and I had to reassure her that in the normal course of events they were invited to parties and were expected to attend. She rang me on several occasions for a chat, obviously feeling lonely, and I was pleased that my party had given her the confidence to contact me. To talk to someone in the same position as yourself is always reassuring.

Unfortunately, the tour began disastrously and didn't get any better; and not only from the cricketing angle.

Not long after it began Bob Willis had to return because of injury and Robin Jackman of Surrey was chosen to replace him. Robin has a South African wife and had obviously spent some time there. The authorities in Guyana, where the team were to play next, stated that because of his South African connections they could not allow him to play in their country. When Ian later told me all about the tour's difficulties, I found this one hard to believe. After all, Geoff Boycott was also on the tour. He too had played in South Africa, but nothing was said about this connection. There didn't seem to be any logic in the actions of the Guyanese government. According to Ian, this seemed to be the hallmark of Guyanese officialdom – no logic at all! Ian, A. C. Smith and Ken Barrington – captain, manager and assistant manager – spent hour after hour in futile discussions and arguments with one official after another, none of whom seemed to know what the discussions were all about. Conflicting instructions were issued from London. All in all it was an anxious and frustrating time. For the team, wanting simply to get on with the game, enforced seclusion within their hotel was hard to bear. They were not actually under house arrest but they had been strongly advised to remain in the hotel. This advice was passed on to the players as an order.

Ian is not easily frightened, but he was fearful here in Georgetown. The team had to have armed guards on their practice days to accompany them to and from the grounds. The numbers of machetes and guns around them made further persuasion to stay indoors unnecessary.

We saw and heard quite a lot of this on news bulletins and I spent an anxious time realizing that a maniac with a gun or a machete and fuelled by a misplaced sense of nationalism could cause untold disaster. No doubt the troubles here were a large contributing factor to what was to follow in Barbados.

My parents, the children and myself joined the team in Barbados and we found ourselves much in demand for television, press and radio interviews. We tried to accommodate the journalists as much as possible while sheltering the children from too much exposure.

The team were pleased to be playing cricket again after their enforced idleness; the weather was glorious, it was lovely to be together again and we spent a few days happily enjoying ourselves. The men would go off to cricket and we would relax on the beach, trying to decide whether the call of the sun and sea was stronger than the call of the cricket. The former was obviously stronger for some of the journalists, and I could name one or two I saw stretched out on the beach writing their match reports from the comments of the West Indian radio commentators. Perhaps this was why their reports always seemed to be biased so strongly against England.

It can't last, I thought, and it didn't. At 7.15 one morning there was a telephone call from team manager Alan Smith. 'Kath, this is Alan. I have some very, very bad news for you. Ken died last night.' Stunned, I passed the receiver to Ian. 'I don't believe it, Ian – Kenny's dead.'

Ian listened for a while, then he dressed in an oppressive silence. 'I'm going to see A. C. [Smith],' he said, 'Get Diane and the children up. Tell your parents what's happened and I'll meet you all in the breakfast room.'

The breakfast room was full of people toying with cups of coffee, no one ate as the news filtered around the hotel. No one could believe it; no one wanted to believe it. Ken Barrington had been very popular with everyone. The suddenness of his heart attack was horrific. It was a very silent team that set off to play cricket that day. I had thought they would cancel the day's play, but it was agreed that Ken would not have wanted that. Both teams stood in silence before play began and, because I know Ian so well, I knew how deeply grieved he was and what he must have been feeling as he stood there with the others.

That evening Ian spent a long time with Ann Barrington, who was due to fly home the next day with her husband's body. They talked of how much Ken had meant to them both.

At a memorial service held later in London Ann asked Ian to read the lesson. He was proud to be asked to do this. He had always asserted that the problems in Guyana caused Ken's premature death.

The tour had to go on. It was decided not to replace Ken, so Ian and Alan Smith were kept busy with the extra work this entailed. This was good for Ian, even though it meant less time spent with us.

I have already mentioned that Geoff Boycott was a member of this tour. I have known Geoff since I was a little girl. I got on as well with him then as my son Liam did years later in Barbados. Liam was four at the time and would go running to meet Geoff whenever he saw him get off the team bus. They would go off together hand in hand to Geoff's room from where a telephone call would come some time later. 'Kathy? Liam is just having a cup of tea with Geoff, we'll bring him back later.' Going round one day to pick up Liam, Anne Wyatt – Geoff's long-time lady friend, said, 'Just come and look at this.' Geoff was stretched out on the bed having discussions with his ghost-writer, Terry Brindle, and balancing a cup of tea on his stomach. Liam was stretched out alongside him in exactly the same position complete with cup of tea. Anne told me that he copied everything Geoff did, even to having his tea sweetened with honey instead of unsweetened as he was used to.

After Barbados, we flew on to Montserrat. This is a very small island and we encountered dreadful problems with accommodation. Many of the wives, including myself, were made to feel responsible for this. During the week Peter Lush, public relations officer for the TCCB, joined us for a meal, together with Alan Smith. We discussed the difficulties of the tour in general and, fortified with a glass or two of wine, I brought up the subject of wives on tour, relating a few of my past experiences and the feelings of some of the other wives. In typical male fashion they kicked the argument around a bit without really committing themselves to any opinion and I realized that although I had Ian's complete support I hadn't made much progress. On the 1986–87 tour of Australia, however, Peter Lush was made manager and, for the first time ever, we were made very welcome indeed.

It was not only the cricketers who had their wives out there, the partners of the press had arrived for the Barbados/Antigua part of the tour. I must admit I was wary of their presence. On the surface they were friendly, but I always felt on my guard with them. This may have been totally unnecessary and, in fact, there was nothing to give foundation to my fears, but they did seem anxious to pick up gossip, particularly any which could have been of national interest.

I am told by some of the more senior and valued members of the press entourage that, in days gone by, relations between journalists and players were much better; each had a mutual respect for the other. Since the advent of the 'circulation war' the problems have intensified. 'News hounds' have infiltrated the authentic cricket writers, and editors at home have demanded startling stories to enliven the more mundane cricket statistics. This has led to a wariness that was never present before. I am sure many of the newspaper men regret this as much as anyone, as they find it more and more difficult to gain, and keep, the trust of the players about whom they are paid to write.

Henry Blofeld wrote a particularly pungent article in the *Sunday Express* about Ian which was critical and cutting in the extreme. A 'friend' (anonymous, of course) sent it to Ian along with an abusive letter. Ian has always regarded Henry as a friend and, being extremely hurt by some of his more personal attacks in the article, tackled him man-to-man about it. As far as both Henry and Ian were concerned, that was that. Unfortunately, their heated exchange had been witnessed and the incident occupied an unwarrantable amount of space in the tabloids, to the regret of them both. Henry has since apologized to both of us for the article.

Relations with the press have been made more difficult for Ian, of course, by his contract to write a weekly article for the *Sun*. Some journalists resent the fact that for this he receives payment in excess of theirs. They may well be correct in their suggestion that cricketers should stick to cricket and leave the writing about it to journalists. Perhaps, though, they forget that a sportsman's career is a short one and that life 'at the top' may be very short indeed, while they can go on writing to a ripe old age.

When Ian was offered this lucrative newspaper contract we were both delighted, not foreseeing the controversy it would bring in its wake. The restrictions it put on his relationships with reporters from other newspapers has caused great problems. At times it seemed as though all the other newspapers were uniting to bring him down, hoping, perhaps, if they could do this that the *Sun* would not continue to rise and shine quite so brightly each weekday morning. It also made life difficult for me as there have often been times when I wished to exclude all journalists, reporters and cameramen from our lives. However, I must say that there have been times when I have been grateful for the protection and help the *Sun* has given us.

The West Indian Tour finished just before the Easter weekend and, because the English cricket season started immediately, our solicitor Alan Herd asked if we would mind turning our annual Easter Lake District holiday into a working one. He knew that once Ian became caught up in the new season there would be no time to discuss the many facets of the Grimsby crown court case which had come to light while Ian had been away.

Ian spent four or five days in the Lakes with us. During a lot of that time closeted with Alan. Then he went to Somerset to begin the home season. Those four or five days gave us a welcome period of relaxation, for immediately afterwards speculation grew apace. Should Botham continue as captain of England after losing the series in the West Indies? It seemed to be the only issue that concerned anyone at this time. Should he even remain in the side? Several of his detractors had a field day on this one. It seemed that every television programme discussed it, newspapers and magazines were full of it, even comedians cracked jokes about the situation. The ultimate indignity was the BBC 2's 'Newsnight' programme which ran a series called 'The Trial of Ian Botham' giving the 'fors' and 'againsts' of Ian remaining captain. In view of the real trial which was to come I felt this was in very bad taste, a sentiment echoed by Mike Brearley in an article in *The Times* in which he condemned whole-heartedly the perpetrator of this idea.

For me Ian put on a brave face, shrugging off the criticism and refusing even to appear to be affected by it, although I knew that he was hurt and, possibly, bewildered by it. I certainly was. I couldn't understand why, since England were expected to lose to the West Indies anyway, Ian should be made the scapegoat. I wonder how many wives would like their husbands' jobs to be analysed so very publicly in all corners of the land.

Now – in the summer of 1981 – we were playing the Australians and, as usual, when the chips are down they really are down. England lost the one-day Internationals – two games to one – and I think at that time I would have been deeply grateful had the selectors announced that a new captain would be selected for the Test series.

At the end of the one-day Test at Headingley, where England lost the series, Ian told me to go on home and he would come later with my father. I sat for a moment contemplating defeat when I saw the convoy of reporters crossing the field for the obligatory captain's press conference. I was forcibly reminded of a firing squad lining up for action with Ian as the victim, and I longed for a hand-grenade. I arrived home not knowing if Ian had been given the captaincy. When he did arrive he said nothing, and I didn't ask him. We were in the kitchen having a drink when it was announced on the news that Ian had been given the captaincy for the first match only. There had been previous discussion in the media about this possibility and I knew how much extra pressure it would put on him. This was followed by the inevitable speeches by invited guests who had obviously been chosen to make provocative statements.

I was weary of listening to my husband being publicly discussed. I had had enough. Turning to him in amazement I said, 'Why didn't you tell me, Ian?' His reply was 'Well, it wasn't worth mentioning it, was it?'

'It's not worth it, Ian. Why don't you give it up?' It wasn't the first time I had thought it but it was the first time I had actually spoken the words out loud.

Nor was it the first time I realized that he had changed: he had become moody and withdrawn. We had several days together and I found that I couldn't talk to him. Either he didn't listen or he didn't want to know. We snapped at the children and at each other, and even Tigger, our faithful boxer dog, took to moping around the house instead of being her usual bouncy self. She did get moments of relief when Ian, in his new solitary mood, took her out for long walks, rejecting all offers of company. Invitations from friends were refused, he just didn't want to do anything. I was dreadfully worried about him and frankly didn't know how to deal with the situation. We couldn't speak openly, and I am sure that he thought he was hiding his feelings from me. When questioned he would say, 'Everything's fine,' and would become very irritated if I questioned further.

When the time came for him to return to Somerset I was relieved, yet I also felt a strong sense of failure. I hadn't been able to help him, nor he me. When I next saw him, before the start of the Trent Bridge Test match, I could see that he was much happier in a male environment. He surrounded himself with other cricketers and close friends, and I was shut out and felt in the way. I was finding it increasingly difficult to be as supportive as I felt I ought to be and, in the end, I decided to stay away.

During this period I lost over a stone in weight, and those who know me will confirm that I couldn't really afford to do this. Ian would ring regularly and I know he was anxious about me. I felt guilty when he asked me to meet him and I refused, giving all sorts of excuses, but I knew deep down that even though he believed he wanted me around, he was happier with his male colleagues. Just as he hadn't come to terms with fame, he couldn't with failure and he didn't want me around to witness it. Even my father, who would normally go through hell and high water for me, was mildly critical of me as he set out to watch a day at the Trent Bridge match. 'Someone must go,' he said. 'We mustn't be fair-weather supporters.' The family kept in constant touch. Les and Marie rang me and my parents frequently. We were all harassed by the situation and all worried for each other.

I can't remember why, but when we heard that Ian had been appointed captain for the Lord's Test – again for only one match – we all decided to go for the whole match. I walked into Lord's determined to keep my head high and passed, tight-lipped, a series of billboards which screamed out 'Botham Must Go' headlines to an article written by John Thickness of the *Evening Standard*. I sat poker-faced and incognito in the crowd, overhearing criticism of Ian from all around me. I also had to listen to wildly inaccurate stories about his private life.

One of the privileges accorded to the wife of an England captain is being invited to the Lord's Box during the Test match. I decided to go then, feeling that there I would be known and could avoid offensive remarks. I was warmly welcomed although I think I was an embarrassment to some people, who didn't quite know what to say when they saw me. With people you meet mostly, or only at cricket matches, there isn't much to talk about except cricket, and that subject was taboo. Small-talk and pleasantries were soon exhausted. When I left I was told that they would be pleased to see me there again, any time I wished to avail myself of the privacy. I was grateful for their thoughtfulness.

From this match I prayed for two things: one, that we should win the match and, two, that Ian would do well. Neither prayer was answered. He didn't bowl too badly but the dreaded 'pair' was his fate when he batted. As he walked back to the pavilion after his second duck the silence was deafening. The MCC members through whose pavilion he had to walk remained impassive, not a hand-clap, or a smile, or a flicker of emotion. A duck usually merits a sympathetic clap or good-natured smiles. Criminals, I am sure, have been accorded better treatment. I saw them as dark-suited vultures who had been waiting for the kill and I have never forgotten or forgiven MCC members for their treatment of Ian.

Utterly miserable, I walked back to the hotel to collect my things and tell Diane to bring the children across to say 'goodbye' to Daddy. It was the last day of the match. England had lost and we were going home.

I was surprised to see so many people still around when we walked back through the Grace Gates at Lord's. Normally at this time there would have been only a few spectators waiting for autographs, and the cleaning staff. However, among the people flocking together I saw familiar faces from the press and television.

Reg Hayter and his wife Lucy came across to us. 'What's going on, Reg? Has something happened?' I inquired. Reg was surprised to be asked this and, rather embarrassed, said that he thought Ian had resigned the captaincy. Mixed emotions flooded through me. I was speechless. Donald Carr joined us and in view of the media interest in our little group, he and Reg decided it would be better to get me away.

Mr Carr took me to the Lord's Box for a drink. He was very kind and hedged around the issue of what had happened because, like everyone else, he felt Ian should be the first to tell me. He spoke very highly of Ian and said the two of us had earned much respect from people over the way we handled a very difficult situation during the last year. It was lovely to hear this, as I had often wondered what the authorities were thinking. We had taken such a hammering over recent months and it seemed that only family and close friends were supporting us. I knew that Ian had enemies in high places but it was encouraging to hear that he still had some friends. It suddenly dawned on me that I had left the rest of the family to wonder what was happening and suggested that we should go to find them. I assured Mr Carr that I was perfectly all right and thanked him for the consideration he had shown me.

The family had been recognized by the television crews who must have realized I would eventually return to them; the numbers hanging around had vastly increased. Spotting one friendly face in the crowd, Alan Lee, a journalist friend, I moved towards him. We talked and I just couldn't believe it when I realized that the sound recordist from ITN had his equipment switched on and poised to catch snippets of our conversation. Alan saw this at the same time and, turning to Tony Francis the sports reporter, said: 'It's just not on, Tony, please have the men move away.' 'Sorry, Kath,' said Tony and they did, in fact, move off.

Ian, holed up in the dressing room, had heard of the trouble I was having and asked Nick Hunter, producer of BBC outside broadcasting sport, to take me to sit in the car in the players' carpark and to get the rest of the family back to the hotel where, he hoped, we could meet up again in privacy. Almost immediately Ian joined me in the car and we were very grateful to Nick Hunter for shielding us from the cameras, both his own and ITN's. I don't remember what exactly Ian told me except that he had resigned the captaincy. I was quite clear in my own mind what I was going to do. I had already arranged with my parents and Diane that they should take the children home and I would go with Ian to the next match in Somerset. They were already back at the hotel reorganizing the luggage.

Ian drove out of Lord's with the gaggle of photographers running alongside the car almost falling over each other in their eagerness for a shot of us together. I told him of my plans. There was a most emphatic, 'No, I want you to go back with the children.' I was completely taken aback, but there was no budging him. He had made up his mind. I was upset and very angry.

Minutes later we pulled into the hotel carpark where the family was waiting. The briefest of goodbyes was said, and off he went. At that moment I hated him; he had spurned the love and support I had offered and dismissed them, it seemed, almost casually.

I knew Ian had done this as a way of sheltering me from any further abuse and harassment, fearful of what might happen the next day, but I felt then, and still do, that I should have been with him. I was left to pick up information about what was happening from the media. As Ian's wife I knew no more than the millions of people switching on their television news programmes that evening.

On our journey home we talked over what we knew of the situation and by the time we arrived I had calmed down a lot. I switched on the 'News at Ten' to hear Alec Bedser, the chairman of the selectors, say that Ian had indeed resigned but that they were going to sack him anyway. After everything that had happened recently, that was the final punishing blow. Surely they could have left him some dignity. They were free to choose another captain, did it matter how that freedom had been gained? Although the remainder of Mr Bedser's speech was kind and intended to further Ian's career we have never forgotten those few fateful words.

Hearing from Ian's parents in Taunton the next day that he had had a wonderful reception there, and hearing his mother say, 'You should have been here, Kathryn,' rubbed salt into my wounds. They couldn't have known, of course, why I wasn't there.

During Somerset's one-day match Ian launched a blistering attack on the bowlers. At his lowest ebb he always seemed to produce a sizzling performance. My sense of isolation was increased when the following day the papers were full of the Botham family enjoying the euphoria of it all while I was 270 miles away. It took me a long time to forgive Ian completely for blocking me out of this part of his life.

Speculation now centred on whether Ian would actually be asked to play during the next Test. As Ian predicted during his 'resignation' interview, Mike Brearley was appointed captain for the remainder of the series. Mike rang Ian prior to the selection meeting to ask him what he felt about playing. This was a thoughtful gesture on Mike's part as it made us realize that some people still had

confidence in Ian. Predictably, Ian was keen to play and I
awaited the team announcement with some trepidation. In
the meantime, I set about answering the vast amount of
supportive mail we had received.

On the Sunday morning we heard that Ian was in the
squad. I was pleased because this is what we had wanted,
but it was to prove an anxious time. All eyes would be on
him to assess his performance. The loss of the captaincy
was a gigantic step backwards down the ladder of success,
would the end of this match see him at the very bottom?

Ian's performance during the first days of this match –
the third Test – was to lift the tension which had surrounded me for so long. Six wickets in an innings, followed
by 50 runs and I could relax, although England were well
on the way to defeat. I am not too proud of the fact that
their imminent defeat didn't upset me too much.

A barbecue, planned during captaincy days, was held
for the team and our friends on the Saturday evening and
it was the first time for many months that we relaxed and
really enjoyed ourselves.

I was actually looking forward to watching Monday's
play. Leaving home I drove towards Headingley, for once
listening to the Test match commentary. Approaching the
roundabout leading on to the motorway, another England
wicket fell leaving us still well behind. I wondered fleetingly whether to drive round the roundabout and return
home to prepare a meal for Ian who, it seemed, would
soon be on his way. I didn't dwell too long on this thought
and continued towards Headingley.

I sat with Jane Border and Angela Wood, two of the
Australian wives. I was happy because Ian had done so
well and they were happy because Australia was winning.
Not long after lunch Ian came in to bat. At this time
Ladbroke's were quoting 500–1 against an England win. It
wasn't until I noticed 30-odd on the board against Ian's

name that I started to take any notice. The crowd was getting noisier, the Australian wives were getting quieter and the atmosphere became electric. The rest is history. Botham 149 not out. Queues outside television shops in town centres followed every ball, factory workshops ground to a halt as radios were turned up, the Stock Exchange ceased trading for minutes, or so it was alleged, and cars stopped in laybys as drivers found the excitement made driving actually dangerous. The next day, unbelievably, England turned defeat into victory and the villain once more became a hero.

Rightly or wrongly Ian refused to attend a press conference which had been hastily arranged. There was no obligation now he was no longer captain and the tenuous thread which holds together player and journalist had long ago been broken. He walked to the Cornhill tent for a celebration drink with a huge blue towel wrapped round his mouth, placed there by Bob Willis as a 'I have nothing to say' sign. I stood proudly waiting for him as a somewhat embarrassed stream of reporters filed past. One or two managed the odd word in my direction, one or two were frankly delighted, the majority obviously didn't know what to say and were not altogether pleased that their dire predictions had been disproved.

The remaining Test matches were equally astounding as far as Ian's performances were concerned. He went from strength to strength and life both on and off the field became rewarding and enjoyable for both of us. Once more I was included in his life. I had tasted the depths, now I was to feast on the heights. For the first time ever I was invited into the dressing-room at Headingley to join the team in their celebration champagne. A jolly crowd of us later enjoyed fish and chips at 'Bryan's' fish restaurant and, this time, we were allowed to eat without people at neighbouring tables reminding Ian about his weight. Little

Liam choked badly on a fish bone and Daddy had to do a rescue act, his second of the day.

The following match at Edgbaston brought me down to earth. Sarah, aged two, had suspected glandular fever. I couldn't go to the match so Ian, with another match-winning performance, finished it off early and spent a happy family day with us at home. Annie Denning and Claire and Sammy, and Sue Breakwell and her two children, James and Donna, were all staying with us. Somerset were playing Yorkshire at Sheffield and this gave the Somerset wives the chance to have a get together. The day consisted of a water slide competition on the lawn. Originally for the children, it became a competition to the death between the adults. Ian walked off with this trophy too! Afterwards he graciously sat us near the paddling pool and plied us with chilled white wine. Lovely, until it became obvious how strategically he had placed the water sprinkler!

A week later, at Manchester, another spectacular century in glorious sunshine also brought the sobering realization that young Liam was receiving too much media attention. He had been seen in photographs and, unknown to us, while playing cricket in the nets with other young boys, had been televised by the BBC for inclusion in 'cricket highlights'. He was beginning to be recognized and when one day we saw him offering his own autograph to the queue surrounding Ian, we thought it expedient to remove him from the limelight for a while.

Sarah, on the other hand, who turned out not to have glandular fever after all, slept her way through much of her time at the matches. She fell asleep one evening under a table in the Cornhill hospitality tent and Ian scooped her up to cradle her gently. Peter Smith of the *Mail* remarked on the contrast between Ian's savage attack on the Australian bowling and the tenderness with which he handled his small daughter.

During August I was approached by a member of the 'This is Your Life' research team. They wanted to do a programme on Ian depending upon the result of the assault trial. This brought me up with a jolt. I had almost forgotten the court case hanging over us. True to form though – 'when you're up you're up – at the end of the three-day trial Ian was cleared of the stigma of having knocked out Steven Isbister's front tooth. In fact, Mr Isbister had lost not only his tooth but also any dignity he might have had. Even the newspapers, who had earlier screamed for Ian's blood over this affair, formed the general consensus that the case should never have come to court.

Following this we enjoyed a short break in California with the bat-maker Duncan Fearnley and Norman Gifford of Worcestershire. It was Norman's benefit tour and a refreshing break for us. During our time there Liam was able to meet his hero of the moment, the 'Incredible Hulk', and Ian, more than most of us, enjoyed his day at Disneyland.

During this time a telephone call confirmed that 'This is Your Life' was to go ahead. Ian had already been selected for the forthcoming tour of India under a new captain, Keith Fletcher of Essex, so it was decided to televise the programme on the eve of the team's departure. On several occasions I nearly called the whole thing off when it became increasingly obvious that the producer wanted to pack the show with celebrities to the exclusion of many who really had influenced Ian's life. It was a complete surprise to him when Eammon Andrews turned up at Lord's. The whole thing went off pretty well in the end, though, and I'm sure he was delighted to be the subject of that week's programme. It was a disappointment to everyone who had taken part in the programme, and the many others who had been invited to the party which followed, that the cricketers were not allowed to stay – not even Ian – because they had to attend an official function, the first of many during that tour.

Life had been full that summer. Reaching the depths and then the heights had taken its toll but, surprisingly, I found it easy to settle after Ian's departure for India. Liam began school full time and immediately took a dislike to it. It was apparent from the early age of four that he had inherited his father's determination. Every morning he was determined not to go to school and we ran the gamut of emotions. I reasoned, cajoled, threatened and despaired until brute force took over. He argued very forcibly as to why, in his opinion, school was unnecessary – except on Wednesdays when they played football in the afternoons. Sarah, on the other hand, joined a play-group and loved it, taking part in all the activities with gusto.

Diane stayed on with us even though the children were now away for most of the day, and I occupied myself with reorganizing the house, having plans drawn up for an extension and enjoying being able to choose new furnishings. The cricket was going well in India and I was looking forward to spending a week or two in India with Ian after Christmas at home with the children. Things were looking good.

9

Making the News

On Boxing Day 1982 I left a foggy, frosty Epworth to fly to Calcutta. I had mixed feelings about going as, for the first time, I was leaving the children behind for more than a day or two, planning to spend three weeks in India.

I found there was much to admire in India, the magnificent architecture, the warmth of the people. It was all magically different to anything I had known before and I loved it. There were many things, though, that I found difficult to understand, knowing little about the politics and religions of India, and I found the immense difference in the way of life between 'the haves' and 'have-nots' incomprehensible.

I was sorry that Ian was not able to join me on these short journeys into a different world. Because the Indians take their cricket so seriously it was inadvisable for players who were instantly recognizable to go sightseeing. Ian, or 'Iron Bottom' as they called him, came into that category. He was treated like royalty, crowds would wait outside the hotel just to see him get into the bus, chanting his name all the while. His popularity kept him a virtual prisoner in the hotel.

We were able to get a day or two's break which we spent at Fisherman's Cove, a seaside resort just south of Madras. Unfortunately, Ian picked up a virus there and became quite ill. We returned to the team hotel in Madras where the combined ministrations of Bernard Thomas, the team physiotherapist, and myself managed to get him fit in time for the Madras Test match. I remember having difficulty obtaining a constant supply of clean dry sheets for the bed, which needed changing every hour or so as Ian was running a high temperature. Every so often he would sit in the bath while Bernard and I sluiced him with body-temperature water. This went on for forty-eight hours. I didn't sleep at all. Feeling much like Florence Nightingale, I was proud of myself when he was pronounced fit enough to do battle in the Madras Test.

Life was going very smoothly. I heard from home that they were doing battle with deep snow and that the children were loving it. Everything was going well in India so it was all the more annoying when a small cloud appeared on the horizon in the guise of two members of the press who warned Ian that 'someone somewhere is out to get you'. They couldn't tell him any more than that because that was the extent of their information.

Following this warning two minor irritations occurred. Ian was accused of brawling in a bar when he hadn't even been there and one evening when we *were* in the bar he was reported to the tour manager and accused of being rude to another hotel guest. It was, in fact, a joke that misfired, perpetrated by another member of the team, and had nothing at all to do with Ian. These were mere pinpricks, though, and didn't seem to be connected with the warning.

Shortly after Ian's return from this tour we were enjoying a rare evening on our own. The children were tucked up in bed when the doorbell rang. On answering Ian was handed a large envelope containing plans for a rather extensive alteration to our home. He was speechless because he knew nothing about them. I had become so independent and used to making all the decisions that I hadn't thought to mention it. He was quite happy about it, though, because the plans included a large games room for him.

Although we thoroughly enjoy spending so much of our time abroad, we still love our family holidays in Britain. Following the India tour, as usual, we spent Easter in the Lake District. Ian and I with the children, my parents and dogs, duly arrived at the flat we rent each Easter to join my sister Lindsay and husband Paul, Brian and Viv Close and their children, plus Alan Herd and family, and various uncles, aunts and cousins. We formed a huge party of family and friends in adjoining flats and had a great time together. Over the years more flats have had to be rented to accommodate our growing families and now a younger generation play happily together.

Each Easter Sunday we organize an Easter-egg hunt for the children and this has become a family tradition. This particular year we decided to take a picnic across to an island in the middle of Lake Ullswater and have the hunt there. There was a minor setback when we discovered that our speedboat, which Dad and Ian had joined forces to buy the year before, needed repairs and a service. Its return was promised for early Sunday morning.

Brian and Viv, and Lynn and Lance their children, set out in their boat and we arranged to join them on the island. As time went on and our boat didn't appear, the children were getting frantic, so Ian suggested that he and Alan should drive us to the layby opposite the island and attract Closey's attention, so that he would come across in his boat to fetch us. In the meantime the men – Ian, Dad, Paul and Alan – would wait for our boat and join us later, bringing the food with them. This seemed a very good idea, so we quickly packed the food for them to bring, gathered up the parcels of small chocolate eggs and set off.

Arriving at the layby we found it occupied by a small car parked neatly in the middle, making it impossible for another vehicle to get either behind or in front of it. Ian muttered a few unintelligible words and started to open the door. 'No!' Alan said in his best solicitor's voice. 'Leave it to me, Ian.' He strolled up to the couple sitting in their car and said, charmingly, 'Excuse me, sir, would you mind pulling your car forward a little so that we can park behind you?'

'Yes, I would mind,' said the driver.

'But we can't park with you in that position,' reasoned Alan calmly.

'I'm not moving an inch,' was the unhelpful reply.

'Sir,' Alan was becoming assertive, 'This layby is intended for at least two, possibly three, cars. Because of the way you are parked no one else can get into it. We are not allowed to stay on the road. I ask you reasonably, please move up a little.'

At that the large lady in the passenger seat leaned across and wagged a finger admonishingly. 'We've come out 'ere to enjoy the view,' she said, 'and that's what we're going to do. We ain't moving for nobody.'

'Madam,' Alan was losing his temper, 'you have no right to take up all the available space.'

They both ignored him.

Defeated, he turned back to us. 'They're bloody mad,' he said in desperation.

'Get in,' said Ian, and he determinedly shunted our car backwards and forwards inch by inch, nosing his way into the space available. When he was almost there the couple in front who had been watching this, first with amazement and then with growing distrust, drove off with a great flurry and grinding of gears. What Ian and Alan said next is unprintable.

We all piled out of the car and scrambled down on to

the lake shore. A large group of rocks to one side provided a landing stage and, after vigorous effort with voice and arms, Brian got the message and set out to pick us up. First the children and I were ferried across the lake, then Lindsay and Mum clutching the parcels of chocolate eggs. In courteously helping Mum into the boat across the slippery rocks Brian stepped into what he thought was a few inches of water to find himself standing thigh-deep with wellingtons well and truly full of icy cold liquid. On our way across it began to sleet.

Arriving at the island Mum and Lindsay set about hiding the eggs in nooks and crannies while we occupied the young ones at the far side. Unknown to us, another family had moored their boat on that side and two young children were having a whale of a time hunting out the eggs. We called Liam and Sarah over and, with the help of Lynn and Lance, who in their mid-teens had passed the stage of wanting to join in, they set about excitedly searching. In stretching up to grab a brightly coloured egg from a cranny in a rock, Liam overbalanced and fell flat into the water. Naturally, all the changes of clothing were to come later in the other boat. Everybody charged across to help pick Liam out of the lake leaving Sarah who, carefully and without any fuss, copied her older brother, thinking the whole thing part of the game. At this point I lost my cool. There we were in the middle of Lake Ullswater in the snow and sleet with two dripping children and no towels or changes of clothing.

Like the old man of the sea Brian was sitting in the lea of some rocks, having lit a fire to dry out his socks which were hanging precariously over a Heath-Robinson-type contraption of sticks being well and truly smoked. He saw us approaching bearing two small wet children, and with supreme optimism shouted, 'I've got a good fire going – come over here, you'll soon dry off.' Viv and Lynn busied

themselves finding suitable spare clothing from their store
and we all sat around the fire sharing the Closes' lunch.
Lance turned suddenly to help himself to another sandwich
and, in doing so, precipitated Brian's socks into the fire. A
stream of colourful language flowed while we all stifled
laughter as he tried to rescue his pair of charred socks.

Hoping that the others would soon arrive with our food,
we busied ourselves collecting wood to keep the fire going,
feeling like modern Robinson Crusoes. As I raised my
head from collecting a particularly chunky piece of dead
wood I noticed a flight bag floating smoothly past on the
ripples of the lake. Looking more closely I saw D. B.
Close written on it and simultaneously heard Viv shout,
'keep the fire going – Brian's fallen in!' In fact he had
tripped over a carelessly laid paddle from a canoe whose
occupants had tied it to a tree and then disappeared, with
several bottles of wine, into the middle of the island. The
paddle snapped in half and we did momentarily wonder
whether it would serve to get the canoe back to the
mainland!

Just about this time Dad and Paul arrived in a small boat
they had hired for the afternoon, worried because we had
no food with us. Our own boat, we were informed, still
hadn't arrived from the repairers. Ian had decided to wait
for it and would join us as soon as possible. I had a mental
picture of Ian ensconced in the comforts of a local hostelry,
enjoying his wait while we battled with the elements. It
was now snowing, the early morning sunshine which had
tempted the expedition having long since gone. We sat
down near the dying fire to eat again, Brian wearing a
strange assortment of clothes, looking like a cross between
a Bedouin and a deep-sea fisherman.

We waited and waited, singing songs and playing games
to keep the little ones amused. I was growing anxious by
this time, imagining Ian at the bottom of the lake. Eventu-

ally we decided we really must make the return journey as it was getting late. We had an eight-mile journey to make in two small boats, one of which had a 40 horsepower engine and seated four people. The other we rudely called a 'put-put', which meant we could have rowed it faster had we had any oars. Brian suggested that we should tie the hired 'put-put' to the back of his boat and he would tow us home to get us there more speedily. Loading operations began. Remembering the country code we carefully put out the last glowing embers of the fire, passed the soggy bundles of clothes and our litter into the boats and began to scramble into them ourselves. Paul perched himself on a rock to help the ladies across while Dad and Brian held the boats steady. In the split second in which Mum was relying solely on Paul for balance, halfway between boat and rock, his foot slipped. With a superhuman effort he threw Mum forward and she landed in a heap at the bottom of the boat while Paul, in agonisingly slow motion, slid gently into the water beneath it, shouting, 'It's my bloody mother-in-law!' as he sank.

We all surged forward to help Paul while Brian struggled desperately to keep the two boats near the island against the tidal waves caused by Paul's sudden entry into the water. 'Never mind Paul!' he shouted 'Is Jan all right?' Jan was convulsed with laughter, lying safely in the bottom of the second boat. Paul was dragged out and disappeared behind a tree to emerge seconds later wearing a spare pair of Lynn's jeans which were much too small for him and two damp towels.

With grim determination the little convoy ploughed up the lake towards Pooley Bridge. Ian did not appear and we grew more and more worried as we became colder and wetter. Eventually we arrived and there on the jetty stood my husband, alive and well and beaming all over his face as he cheerfully waved to us. I was furious and said so.

'Before you go on,' he said, 'listen to what I have to say,' and proceeded to unfold a sequence of events almost as ludicrous as our own.

The speedboat had arrived much later than expected and Ian and Alan together with Sarah, Alan's daughter, had decided to try it out before coming to the island. Alan and Ian in the front were speeding along the lake when Sarah, a lively ten-year old, informed them that there was water in the back. 'Oh, that's OK,' said Ian, 'it always takes in a little, don't worry about it.' 'But should it be over my knees?' inquired Sarah. On investigation it was discovered that the bung had not been replaced and the boat had taken in water fast. This meant it had to be winched out of the lake and dried out. Ian was just about to set out to join us when we appeared.

We trailed back to the flat for hot baths and warm food, leaving behind Ian and Dad who decided to try out our boat in case its immersion had caused any problems. As we drew away in the cars we heard the boat zoom up the lake. Some time later, when we were again wondering what had happened, a sheepish pair returned. 'Sorry we're late, but we ran out of petrol in the middle of the lake and had to be rescued!'

Not all our holidays are as eventful as this but all of them are very enjoyable. Over the years we have made a lot of friends in the areas we visit and we look forward to seeing them each year.

Ian is one of those people who will have a go at anything, an all-rounder in the true sense of the word. When an invitation came asking him if he would like to fly with the Red Arrows he didn't hesitate for a second and a date was fixed for him to spend a day at RAF Kemble where this crack flying team were based at the time. Together with Liam and Andy Withers, who had just begun working for

Togetherness: the summer of the ban (1986)

LEFT: Grandpa 100 not out (1986) *Phil Callaghan*
BELOW: A gathering of the clans (my parents, with Liam, to the left, Ian's parents to the right) *Daily Mirror*

Father and son, summer 1986: sound advice, perhaps? *Sunday Mirror*

LEFT: 26 October 1985:
where the Big Walk in aid
of leukaemia research
began. Journalist Frank
Keating on the left, piper
John Macrae on the right
Graham Morris
BELOW: The Duchess of
Kent presents the Gold *Star*
Award for Ian's charitable
work on behalf of
leukaemia victims

Ian as his PA, he sped down the motorway while Sarah and I made plans to join them the next day – to watch.

When I arrived I found Andy very relieved to see me; young Liam had proved rather a handful as he grew more and more excited. Ian had just flown off, literally this time, for a practice run to ensure that, physically, he was up to a full-scale show. The press were arriving in force and television cameras were being set up. Looking up to see the red jet streaking across the sky I hoped that he was enjoying it. Liam and Sarah were hopping about with excitement and there was no doubt Liam would have joined them given half a chance. When the plane landed and taxied to a halt there was a moment or two before anyone appeared, then Ian and the pilot emerged and walked towards the buildings. No one else would have noticed but I thought Ian didn't look too well. He managed a smile for the cameras and a few words, then disappeared. I heard later that the 'G' suit which is worn to offset the effects of gravity was not working correctly, so Ian had been subjected to a test flight without any protection, and consequently was feeling extremely ill. It was almost decided to cancel the flight but Ian insisted that he would be all right next time with a proper suit. Much to everyone's relief, the full-scale practice show went off as planned.

We watched in disbelief as the planes twisted and turned and climbed and dived. I knew which plane Ian was in and watched its progress closely. Liam promptly decided he no longer wanted to play cricket when he grew up, and that he would join the RAF instead.

We became friendly with John Blackwell, the Red Arrows' leader at that time, and his wife Jane. Jane and I led similar lives, with husbands in the limelight and often away from home, and we found we had much in common. I remember once introducing John to some other friends, saying, 'This is John Blackwell, from the Red Arrows.' 'Nice to meet you,' was the reply, 'How do you enjoy pub life then?' Red faces all round!

Another family time we all enjoy is our annual Scottish holiday. Since 1973, each October, at half-term, we stay in Forestry Commission log cabins. At first it was just my family, four of us and a dog, fitting comfortably into one log cabin. Now, with two extra men, five young children and three more dogs, we book two each year. Some years we book even more because Ian's Mum and Dad, sister Wendy and her husband have also joined us. The men play golf, go fishing, stalking, join friends for a drink in the evening, before returning for a good meal prepared by us. The women shop, cook, look after the children and take the dogs for walks. Sounds familiar? We love it, though, and I am exaggerating slightly as I have recently taken up golf, Liam goes fishing with Daddy and most evenings we all join in the pre-meal drinks.

The winter tour of 1982–83 was to Australia. We decided that the ideal thing was to rent a house in Sydney. I didn't intend to follow the cricketers around Australia but the itinerary showed us that Sydney would be their base for much of the time. The children were young enough to miss school, although we went armed with a programme of work prepared by Liam's teacher. We found a pleasant house just five minutes from the team's hotel, and the team manager, Doug Insole, kindly allowed Ian to stay with us when in Sydney.

We thought Sydney was a beautiful city and the children loved the beaches. We held open house at 58 Wallaroy Road, Woolhara and I became skilled at stretching family meals for five to feed ten, fifteen or even more. My humble shepherd's pie was pronounced the best meal ever by a team tired of hotel food.

We have always enjoyed seafood and quickly found

Doyle's at Wasons Bay. Ian and Peter Doyle became good friends and Peter, Ian and Liam spent many happy hours fishing. One of our favourite beaches was Camp Cove. We found it good for children and we could relax, and it had the virtue of being close at hand. The first time we went there we parked the car close to the steps leading down to the beach. Liam with his bucket and spade dashed on ahead, then stopped in his tracks, spread his arms wide and turned to me. 'Mummy!' he shouted in a horrified voice, 'Don't look, there are lots of rude ladies here.'

New Year's Eve was spent in Sydney and we had all been invited to a quayside restaurant/nightclub. We were undecided about going but in the end went for an hour or two to join in with other members of the team. We left some time before midnight, exchanging greetings with some of the Australian team who were just arriving. The next thing we heard about this was a telephone call from Alan Herd informing us that headlines in the English *Sun* newspaper read, 'Botham in New Year's Eve Brawl with Aussie Test Star'. The 'Aussie Test Star' was Rodney Hogg who was as upset as Ian about this story. Eventually the paper issued an apology. I think it was printed on page 17 and took up about three lines.

In Sydney we met Elton John for the first time. We had been invited to Doyle's for a luncheon and he was there. Because the children were enjoying themselves so much on the beach we stayed on longer, as did Elton, and it seemed natural to ask him home with the others for a cup of tea. He played football with Liam for a long time and then came into the kitchen to check that the kettle was on. This was the beginning of our friendship.

The Australian tour was not a cricketing success for Ian and once more there was speculation about his place in the England side. At first this didn't worry us too much. The centuries and five-wicket hauls were eluding him at the moment, but we had no real doubts that his true form would return. Eventually, of course, the whole thing began to get out of hand again. The 'weight problem' reared its ugly head again and there were inferences that he was no longer taking the game seriously and was getting too big for his boots. Ian was getting a lot of knocks but his confidence did not allow him to stay down: as always he sprang back for more. The newspapers and Ian became like opponents in a boxing ring. The more Ian came back with a passable performance, the harder they hit him. All-rounders to take his place were being heralded in all the counties and he was consigned to the scrap-heap times without number.

This is all very well, but my confidence is not as great as Ian's. I knew like all sportsmen's wives that to be pushed on to the scrap-heap at twenty-seven means there is a long time left to support your family – contrary to newspaper reports we hadn't, and haven't, made anywhere near a million. To add to that, I had again become pregnant. Liam was five and Sarah four, and they looked forward to a new brother or sister. As before, the early days of pregnancy did not find me in the best of health. It was not a good time to be pregnant; feeling so ill, the constant stress of media attention was almost impossible to bear.

Ian had been selected for the 1983 Headingley Test match against New Zealand though many thought he shouldn't be, so I set about preparing the by now traditional barbecue. Mike Gibson, the ex-Irish Rugby Union captain, and his wife and family were staying with us. The full house and preparations for the party gave me plenty with which to occupy myself. I was beginning to feel a little better, forcing myself to realize that life had to go on. Therefore it was a terrible shock to be told during a routine ante-natal check that the baby's heartbeat couldn't be heard. I was told this wasn't entirely unusual but could sense that my obstetrician was not happy about the situation. She made the earliest possible appointment for me to have a scan and I went home to 'sit it out' for the weekend. I prayed that Ian would do well at some stage of the match so that everything around was not gloom and doom, but unfortunately it doesn't always work that way. I wondered whether or not to tell him about the baby, knowing he was already under a great deal of pressure. In fact I didn't tell him until he walked through the door the following evening. Then I just knew he had to be told. I might have been telling him that I'd had a bump in the car. 'Don't worry about it,' was all he said.

Later that evening I slipped away from the gaiety of the party and sat alone in the kitchen. Bob Willis came in. 'Are you OK, Kath?' he inquired. 'Ian's told me about the baby.'

'Is *he* all right, Bob? I don't understand his reaction, it's as though he hasn't really heard what I said,' I countered.

'He doesn't know what to say to you. He's bloody upset.'

The Test match finished early which made it possible for Ian to accompany me to obtain the result of the scan. I was advised that I should enter hospital immediately because the baby was dead. I had come to terms with the fact that this might happen and was happy to let Ian take over all the arrangements. He was absolutely marvellous and, having seen me into hospital, organized a plane to Sussex where he captained Somerset in a one-day match. He suddenly found form, taking six quick wickets, which enabled the match to be over by about three in the afternoon and he was back at my side by teatime.

One of the things we wanted above all was to keep this part of our lives to ourselves. It was a private grief and we both felt that it was no business of anyone else. It had been arranged that I should go into hospital as Mrs Baker in the hope that I could remain anonymous. It was a vain hope. Ian's sudden return to form had fired the press's imagination, and I suppose his flying to and from the ground had aroused suspicion. However it came out is immaterial; suffice it to say that the next day the papers were full of it. I had even relegated Mrs Thatcher's eye operation to page 2. BBC news announced at 9 p.m. that I had lost the baby. In fact, that didn't happen until 10.30. News indeed!

It took a long, long time to get over the loss of this baby. Many people expressed the opinion that I shouldn't worry as I had two healthy children already. This didn't help me at all. Each baby is precious and this one would have been equally so. Lindsay and Paul were expecting their first baby the following November and seeing her so obviously blooming was, at first, difficult for me. She told me later how guilty she felt that she was so fit after what had happened to me. Both Ian and I took great delight in her little boy, Tom, when he duly arrived and were pleased and proud to become his godparents.

Immediately following the end of the 1983 cricket season, which saw a revival of form on Ian's part and therefore his selection for the winter tour of New Zealand and Pakistan, we were invited to spend a few days in the south of France with our good friends Alan and Ray Dyer. Alan and Ian had met when Ian was learning to fly. Ian had expressed a wish to fly round the world and Alan was more than willing to go with him as he had already done this once. This time, however, Alan flew us to France in his private plane and we spent five carefree days at their villa.

We returned to England in the knowledge that we would have a good time at home together, as the New Zealand tour didn't begin until after Christmas. Ian became involved with Scunthorpe United again and this season eventually reached the dizzy heights of the first team. The

TCCB were not too thrilled about this and did, in fact, demand that he shouldn't play after the middle of December in case of injury. Ian pointed out that as his contract for the winter tour was dated as beginning some time in January he felt free to do as he liked until that date. Again there was a furore but I didn't let it worry me, though I found it a minor irritation that, at the same time, David Gower and Allan Lamb were abroad skiing and Mike Gatting was also playing football for his local team. Nothing was said about this by the press or the TCCB who probably didn't know about these activities. I have always said that there seems to be one rule for Ian and different rules for the rest – a sentiment shared by many of his team-mates. In 1986, during his ban from first-class cricket, a story appeared in the national press concerning cricketers drinking in a wine bar till all hours prior to a Test match. Ian rang up to reprimand them jokingly and he was told to get back into the team quickly; they wanted someone to take the spotlight away from them again!

It had almost, but not quite, reached the stage where Ian had to choose between playing over New Year's weekend for Scunthorpe or going on the winter tour. I think his name was again placed on the TCCB disciplinary list but, in fact, he heard nothing more about it and eventually set off for New Zealand after presenting me with a 'surprise' Christmas present, a Great Dane puppy which I named Kiri. She was to replace our boxer Tigger who, to our great sorrow, had been killed by a speeding car during the autumn.

The dedication to Scunthorpe was continued by Liam in his father's absence. The club were very good to us and continued to send us tickets for games, even though Ian was no longer playing with them. Liam was eager to be the club mascot for a match and he duly wrote to ask to be considered for this honour. He was thrilled when he

eventually received the coveted invitation to attend the
evening match against Port Vale and act as mascot and ball
boy.

So the winter went on, settling into its usual pace and
fairly peaceful tenor. There was nothing to suggest the
turbulent time which was soon to follow.

On 8 March 1984 news from New Zealand and Pakistan
began to filter through and brought about the most
dreadful period of our lives. All that had gone before faded
into insignificance over the next few months.

It was 'alleged' – that word still haunts me – that eight
members of the England touring team had been taking
drugs and that some members had been seen with 'other
women'. Lurid stories appeared in the tabloids, each one
trying to outdo the other. Once again our telephone and
front doorbell were assaulted by news hounds, and flocks
of photographers lurked around the gate. Once again my
parents took up residence with me to ward off the worst
of the flak. Once again I had to smile for Liam and Sarah
and pretend that everything was fine and dandy and once
again I had to get a grip on myself and force myself to
walk to the shops, greeting my friends and acquaintances
with my head held high and pretending that I really didn't
care what was being said or written.

Anyone who has been the target of virulent press articles
will know the sickening knotting of the stomach when
meeting others. Which of your friends is going to believe
some of it; or even all of it? As you walk round the
supermarket you imagine that everyone is, has just been,
or is about to talk about you, and what you really hate is
pity. Oh, how I dislike the words, 'I do feel sorry for you,
Kathryn', however kindly meant.

During this time Ian and I made frequent telephone calls
to each other and during one of them Ian asked me to get

in touch with Lindsay Lamb, Allan's wife, with whom I was very friendly. Allan, like Ian, is outgoing and friendly and these two were receiving the blackest headlines and the most publicity. Mention of Lindsay pulled me up with a jerk and I suddenly realized that this time there was another wife who was suffering in the same way, for the same reason.

I telephoned her. On reflection I should have got into the car and driven over, and we could have cried on each other's shoulders. The telephone call was not a success; it had come too late, I think. I put the receiver down, trembling and upset because she had castigated me for not contacting her sooner. She pointed out that I had my family to help and support me while her family were in South Africa, and that she had had to face the problems alone. I also felt that she blamed Ian for all the trouble as he and Allan were so friendly and stuck together on tour. At this time I felt sure Lindsay believed in the old adage 'No smoke without fire', and that there was perhaps some truth in the stories (I know Allan had been stricken and upset by some of her telephone calls to him). I can't remember what I replied, but some of it may not have been too friendly.

I think it was the only time I broke down in tears. I was hurt and indignant and worried for our friendship, as I know Allan's friendship is important to Ian.

As I lay awake that night, I suddenly saw myself clearly. I appeared to be standing outside myself looking on, and some of what I saw I didn't like. Perhaps I had hardened over the years, living in the shadows next to Ian in the limelight. I think it is possible that my parents had been *too* supportive. Perhaps they should have occasionally disagreed with my assessment of events and people. I don't know. But I do know that the relationship between Lindsay and me had been subtly but irrevocably bruised by the troubles. We are still good friends, but fire doesn't always temper steel – sometimes it damages or tarnishes it slightly – and through no fault of our own and I believe to our sorrow, we have drifted away from each other in recent years.

The next evening Ian telephoned to tell me he was coming home from Pakistan for an exploratory operation on his knee, which had been troubling him on and off for some considerable time. Bernard Thomas, the tour physio, had decreed that he must return to England immediately for specialized treatment or an operation.

At last, I thought, we can face the world together! The children were excited by Daddy's imminent return although Liam, particularly, realized that all was not well. He had received a fair amount of harassment from the older children at school, and at the age of six was rapidly learning that having a famous Daddy can be a grave disadvantage at times. At least one of his schoolfriends had been told by his mother not to play with 'that Botham child – his family are drug addicts'.

Ian was due home on the Sunday and, because it was my birthday, I had previously arranged to visit a friend in London and to go to the theatre. In view of Ian's arrival I decided to take the children along to meet Ian at Heathrow, banking on the fact that London was as good a place as any in which to hide, and that I could get away from the telephone and the doorbell for a while.

We stayed with Chrissie Garbutt, a feature writer on the *Daily Mirror* and one of the few members of the press that I trusted. Hope began to grow in me that the stupid stories from abroad would dry up. I realized that the meeting at the airport would be difficult because of the media attention and, having heard nothing from Lord's, I asked my father to come with me. Believe me, a woman with two young children needs protection from certain members of the press.

Chrissie, my parents, Liam, Sarah and I enjoyed a good day in London. I began to relax. Soon Ian would be home and all would be better, if not quite well.

On the Saturday evening I received two telephone calls. One was from Donald Carr who said, 'Once tomorrow is over, the worst will be over.' I wondered vaguely what he meant, but was more concerned with his next words: 'Do you think it necessary for anyone from the TCCB to be at Heathrow tomorrow to meet Ian?' I really couldn't believe that Donald Carr would be ringing just for this. Of course I expected someone to be there. Surely they would realize that their presence was vital to show support for Ian at this troubled time. Apart from the fact that when other cricketers came home early because of injury, selectors and other officials from the TCCB always met them, according to the television cameras anyway. Then anger took over. I must have sounded very brusque when I snapped, 'Yes, of course I do. In any event I need help as well.' 'But won't your family be there?' he asked.

The second telephone call was from my distraught grandmother who had had several calls from the *News of the World*. She had steadfastly refused to tell them where I was, in spite of pressure and those verbal arm-twistings that only the press know how to apply. The final attempt had finally broken her: the reporter said, 'We *must* get hold of Kathryn. The *Mail on Sunday* are printing a dreadful piece about Ian and we want to print his side of the story.' Grandma Hind is wonderful at fending off unwanted attention but at this she promised to contact me and ask if I wished to liaise with them.

My heart plummeted at this piece of news. What could be more dreadful than what had already appeared? Of course, I had no intention of contacting the *News of the*

World. I had learned that you do not go willingly to a newspaper on these occasions. The twistings and machinations of reporters were all too familiar to me. However carefully you choose your words they really can rewrite and rearrange and, hey presto, they have you saying anything they want you to say. Also, I sometimes wonder if the faceless beings who write the headlines ever actually read the stories underneath.

Sunday morning dawned after a dreadful night's sleep. Chrissie had arranged a champagne breakfast to celebrate my birthday. I felt absolutely drained but tried hard to join in with Liam and Sarah who were thoroughly enjoying the 'party'. Two reporters from the *Daily Mail* arrived at Chrissie's flat and I derived wry amusement from listening to a *Daily Mirror* journalist telling the *Daily Mail* reporters that Mrs Botham was not at her flat, and that even if she were she would not be available for comment. It didn't occur to me even then to wonder how they had found my hideaway.

Amazingly it began to seem like any other Sunday morning. We dashed about getting ready to be at the airport, Liam and Sarah becoming more and more excited. Chrissie takes most of the Sunday papers but my mother and I refused to read them. If my father knew what was in them, he kept a discreet silence and did an excellent job of behaving as if nothing unusual was going on.

We arrived at Heathrow to find that the flight was delayed by an hour. Walking into the arrival lounge I was astonished by the number of people there with cameras and notepads. Television cameras were there as well. At first I refused to believe that they could only be there for Ian's arrival but, judging by the furtive looks and the faint hum of excitement as we walked in, I soon realized that they were waiting for us.

Donald Carr was already there. As a person, he has

always been helpful and pleasant to me. As a representative of the TCCB, wearing his official hat, he is less so. He was compassionate and kind on this occasion and firmly refused to let the press or television get too close, although it seemed that several miles of film were being taken. He took me on one side to advise me not to give any interviews. I already had decided on this. Then we joined the family for a cup of coffee in the middle of the coffee area at Heathrow. It became a public exhibition. We were in the centre, there was a large no-go area surrounding us and the press prowled around the walls. Looking back, there must have been many ordinary travellers wondering what on earth was going on, but I don't remember anyone else being there!

The plane landed and we waited for Ian to clear passport and customs and at last we spotted him pushing his trolley up the walkway. I moved forward hand-in-hand with our children. Simultaneously the cameramen and reporters surged around us. Little Liam clung tightly to my hand, pushing vainly at people's bodies with his other arm. I heard Sarah crying as she was pushed and buffeted away from me. Over it all one reporter or cameraman shouted, 'For God's sake mind the kids!' Mum said later that she was pulled out of the way by a kindly Heathrow porter who, not knowing who she was, said 'Careful, love – look at those B's. I hope he hits the first one that reaches him.' Her silent prayer was, 'I hope he doesn't!'

Then Ian was up to us and past us. He hadn't seen me or the children or, if he had, the impetus of the crowd had taken him right past us. I rounded up the children and trotted meekly after him, unsure of what to do. He must have suddenly realized what had happened because he stopped, turned and gave us each a somewhat perfunctory kiss which was eagerly photographed by the surrounding hordes. The authorities had allowed my father to park his car away from the main parking area, and Ian, myself, Liam, Sarah, my mother and father and Ian Jarrett, the inevitable *Sun* journalist, plus piles of luggage, packed the Saab 900. In spite of the worry we collapsed into giggles as the car sped through the London streets. Suddenly we realized we were being followed and my father was exhorted to put his foot down. Liam was right when he announced with great glee that it was like being in 'The Dukes of Hazzard'. It was such an anticlimax when we realized that the car belonged to Ian Jarrett and that the driver was trying to keep up with us simply so that Jarrett could eventually go home in it when he had finished his article with Ian.

As we drove down the A1 home to Epworth we talked a lot about what had been written in the press over the previous weeks. Much had been filtered through to New Zealand but Ian had really had no idea of the enormity of it all. The crowds at Heathrow had surprised him, but it had all been somewhat dream-like – almost as if it wasn't really happening to us.

Almost as soon as we arrived home, at Ian's request Dad produced the *Mail on Sunday* from wherever he had been hiding it and Ian retreated to the smallest room in the house to read it. When he emerged I took one look at his face and if I had ever had any doubts they vanished. There was no guilt or fear written there but pure anger. He raged and ranted for a while and then the storm subsided. He rang Alan Herd and arranged a meeting at our home for the next day.

When Alan arrived my job was to supply cups of coffee, tea and, on occasions, something stronger. They went through the report word by word. During this day a feeling of resentment began to grow. In the preceding days I had suffered mentally to an enormous degree, I had staunchly defended Ian against anything anyone had to throw and now here I was reduced to the role of tea-maker. I was allowed no part in the discussion which, in fact, ceased whenever I appeared. I felt bitter. The men were together handling everything in their way to my exclusion. I needed desperately to be a part of it, to be asked for an opinion, to know what was happening or what was going to happen. I wanted more than the snippets of information which they saw fit to give me. I knew I deserved to be a part of it. I was ready to fight but I needed to be allowed to help draw up the battle plans.

Looking back on this I realize that their hearts were in the right places, but they were doing the wrong thing even though it was for all the right reasons.

I remember being vaguely surprised that one of the things which most annoyed Ian was the fact that it was hinted that he hadn't returned for a knee operation at all, but that he had been sent home for disciplinary reasons. However, only forty-eight hours after his return, we were seen on television reporting to a Birmingham hospital where the operation was carried out and all the newspapers carried pictures of Ian with enormous padding and bandages around his knee sitting up in bed surrounded by pretty nurses!

I stayed in Birmingham with Juliette Willis, Bob's wife, who is one of my favourite people, and between us we managed to keep our spirits up. Sacks of get-well cards and presents arrived at the hospital and at home, and the telephone was kept busy. Not one inquiry or card or any form of good wishes came from Lord's. They didn't seem to care whether the operation had been a success or not, even though it had been necessitated by the constant pounding his knee had taken from playing for Somerset and England. Neither of us mentioned it then, but in later months we were to talk about this and realize how much it influenced Ian's attitude towards 'the cricketing authorities'. Perhaps it was at this time Ian realized how little they really thought about people as people. Or perhaps it was then he realized he was on his own. The media were against him because he was almost too successful and the authorities didn't like him because they thought he was becoming bigger than the game.

In fact, there *was* a telephone call from Lord's. During the weekend following Ian's operation I answered a call from Donald Carr. At last! I thought and passed the receiver to Ian, only to hear him exclaim in anger.

Immediately after his operation, still hazy from the anaesthetic, Ian had obliged a friend, Pat Murphy of BBC radio, with a half-hour interview for Saturday morning's 'Sport on 4'. During the interview he was asked about touring conditions in Pakistan. Ian summed it up as just the place to send your mother-in-law on an all-expenses-paid holiday. Everyone, including his mother-in-law, took it for what it was – a joke. Everyone, that is, except Lord's.

The telephone call was to ask Ian to explain his remarks about Pakistan with a view to deciding whether or not there was to be a disciplinary hearing. I well remember Ian's concluding remark: 'By the way, Donald, in case any of you — at Lord's *are* interested, my knee is recovering well and I hope to be fit to start the season.'

My mother often remarks that she must have the only son-in-law to have been officially fined – £1,000 – for joking about his mother-in-law.

The days while Ian was recovering passed slowly. He is a bad patient and finds it difficult to sit around doing nothing. Videos poured in and out of the house and when Ian wasn't closeted with these he spent his time plaguing me in the kitchen, prowling around while I was cooking or washing up. After one meal I found myself with a seemingly endless supply of dirty pots until I caught him slipping the clean ones back among the unwashed ones to be done again. *He* thought it was funny but, having been faced that morning with a non-functioning dishwasher as well as a broken washing machine, I was definitely not amused.

During this time, as originally planned, we flew to Jersey for a day or two and were at Heathrow to meet the rest of the team back from the tour. Also there was Lindsay Lamb. We were rather strained, but otherwise the meeting passed off reasonably well.

If Lindsay still had any doubts about the reliability of newspaper reports, next morning's papers should have dispelled them. Lindsay and Allan had no children at that time but Lindsay had taken her small niece, Lucy, to the airport. Most of the next morning's tabloids bore a large banner headline, 'Welcome Home, Daddy', with a picture of Lindsay, Allan and niece Lucy.

We spent three extremely enjoyable days in Jersey, during which time Ian hired a plane to take us to Alderney to see John Arlott. It was the first time I had met him and I found him charming. I was very much in awe of him as I knew him to be such a respected man in cricket circles and knowledgeable about so many things. How could I, a twenty-nine-year-old housewife, possibly be of any interest to him? He was the complete gentleman and put me at ease immediately. Both Ian and I enjoy seeing him whenever we are able.

As time went on the traumatic events of March, when allegations about drugs and sex had been levelled at half the touring party and specifically at Ian and Allan Lamb, receded only slightly in my mind. However hard I tried, they accompanied my every waking thought. I succeeded in behaving normally with the children and, I think, they soon settled into their usual routine. Ian has an ability to bury anything that is not a burning issue, so everyone around him is driven to distraction by his refusal to talk, or even think, about what is past or what is to come. He

wouldn't talk to me and he didn't want to talk to Alan
Herd; thus I found myself in the unhappy position of go-
between, a circumstance with which Alan and I are not
unfamiliar.

Ian's knee operation was successful and he was able to
start the 1984 cricket season punctually. At this time an
announcement was made that he intended to sue the *Mail
on Sunday*. All the correct legal procedures were under-
taken and the action was set in motion.

Just as the season was about to begin a friend, who was
very dear to both of us, died suddenly. The loss of Pete
McCombe was keenly felt by many of the Somerset team.
His unswerving loyalty, particularly to Viv Richards and
Ian, had meant a great deal to all of us. My visits to the
county ground at Taunton will never be the same: Pete
was one of the few people who was as considerate towards
me as towards Ian. At the time of his death I realized how
much Ian would miss him. Pete had often been Ian's
sounding board and in him Ian had always found a ready
listener and confidant. Sadly, his place by Ian's side has
never been filled in quite the same way, and I know Ian
still misses him.

As the 1984 season was Ian's benefit year, I saw even
less of him than usual. It was an anxious time for many
reasons, not least of which was the fact that we had been
warned by Alan Herd to take great care that we gave no
one an opportunity to plant drugs on us. Cars and car
boots had to be locked at all times. Garages, outhouses,
our home, hotel rooms, Ian's cricket bags, suitcases and
holdalls had to be carefully checked and hidden. To this
day, an independent witness checks his luggage before
going through an air- or sea-port.

Another anxiety was whether he would be chosen for
England. We were delighted that the selectors at least had
kept faith with him when we heard his name in the squad
for the one-day series under a new captain, David Gower.

Although Ian had a successful season, taking nineteen wickets and scoring 347 runs against the West Indies, it was to prove a very frustrating time. I chose not to go to many Test matches so during my days at home I spent much time tuning in to 'Test Match Special' on Radio 3. It seemed that every time I listened either Christopher Martin-Jenkins or Don Mosey were discussing with other members of the commentary team or guests whether or not Ian was a disruptive influence, inferring he was undermining David's captaincy. England were being thrashed, so I assume they were having to find reasons for this and, as usual, were pinning the blame on Ian. As his performance was satisfactory they needed to find something else to jibe about. It angered me to hear Don Mosey talking about members of the side as if he was a good friend to them, misleading the British public because, as I well knew, few members of the team, if any, would speak to him.

Another incident occurred following one of the few breaks Ian had at home with us. He had set off in good time to play in a benefit match at Sparkford in Somerset and had been badly delayed by road works. Arriving a little late he quickly settled down to signing autographs and chatting to groups of spectators. The *Sunday People* carried a frightful story about the match informing people that Ian had refused to sign autographs, had deliberately got himself out and had generally behaved in a churlish manner.

Ian's parents rang to put my mind at rest, saying that none of this was true. They had been there the whole time and everyone concerned with the organization of the match had been delighted. Somerset County Cricket Club supported Ian over this, as indeed they frequently have done.

Sniping by the press continued throughout the benefit

year, causing several sponsors of benefit functions to withdraw their support and, no doubt, many members of the public as well.

As the press at this time were following Ian constantly how the next incident was kept from them is nothing short of a miracle.

Ian had been invited to take part in Terry Wogan's show in October. He had a meeting in London prior to this with his agent Reg Hayter, and I was meeting him there with clothes which, because of his colour blindness, I had newly bought for him to wear. As I watched him try them on he appeared to be very unsteady and awkward in his movements, and I fleetingly wondered if he was ill.

The trousers were impossible, he couldn't get them above his knees. So there he was, in jeans and a T-shirt and the Wogan show a couple of hours away! The meeting was somewhat abridged and a shop called Tommy Nutters in Savile Row was recommended to us. We quickly chose a sweater and trousers, which had to be altered. The staff were marvellous and they rapidly turned what could have been an embarrassing situation into a successful one. Sitting in the hospitality room sipping a gin and tonic, watching Ian chat calmly with Terry, I giggled quietly to myself thinking of the previous two hours' panic. But the panic had stopped me from noticing that Ian really was rather strange.

On the train home, relaxing over a British Rail dinner, Ian related the reason for his drawn appearance. The previous day he had hosted a benefit shooting day in Somerset. Having tramped the fields all day he was relaxing with the other participants over drinks in the country pub where a dinner was to be held as the finale to the shoot.

After only a couple of drinks Ian began to act as though he had drunk two bottles and Andy Withers, realizing something was wrong, quickly crossed to Ian to hear him say, 'For God's sake, Andy, get me out of here.' This he did, only to have Ian crash face forward on to the carpark. To quote Andy; 'I was panic-stricken. I thought he was dead. He was foaming at the mouth and was totally in a different world.' The shoot organizer was extremely helpful; he quickly realized that Ian's drink had been spiked and arranged for Andy to get Ian to bed with haste and secrecy. Andy sat up all night with Ian, desperately worried, not daring to get a doctor for fear of the consequences in the light of recent allegations. This was somebody's sick joke that had gone terribly wrong. It was days before Ian recovered from this and weeks before he could take a drink in a public place with any confidence.

10

An Arresting Incident

It had been an extremely busy English season. Because of the benefit, I had seen even less of Ian; virtually all his free time had been taken up dashing all over the country to functions that had been arranged for him. He was very conscientious about turning up to everything that he knew had been organized but there were one or two problems which arose after Pete McCombe's death. Pete had agreed verbally to a few functions which we knew nothing about; later on, when final arrangements were sent to us, we found Ian had been double-booked. I don't think Ian worked at his benefit with as much dedication as he gives to most things. He doesn't enjoy formal dinners, discos and such like. The many sporting occasions which were organized for him were a different kettle of fish, however. He threw himself into all these with great enthusiasm – golf, fishing, shooting-matches, as well as cricket. I went along to as many as possible, and he had no problems in getting other personalities to turn up to support him. He has always been more than ready to help other people in their benefit year, so they, in turn, turned up in droves to help him.

The biggest drawback to a bumper benefit sum was Ian's generosity! One of the functions arranged was a pro-am golf tournament in conjunction with Geoff Boycott whose benefit year it also was. The proceeds were to be split down the middle and paid into their respective benefit funds. For some reason Geoff was unable to attend, but Ian was there, having taken along with him most of his England colleagues. When, some days later, the cheque arrived together with the statement of accounts the sum raised had been neatly halved, but on Ian's side there had been a hefty subtraction for a bar bill. As usual, Ian had treated everyone in sight as a thank-you. Ian and Geoff had several functions together. Gregarious Ian would always be there at the end, chatting to the organizers, ordering drinks, and often food, for all the helpers, while Geoff's car would be speeding away out of the carpark.

A benefit year runs from 1 January to 31 December. As Ian had been in New Zealand until almost April he had a late start, so his organizer was looking to the winter months to make some real money. 'I don't want you to arrange anything at the weekends,' declared Ian, 'I hope to play football for Scunthorpe again!' Steve, his benefit organizer, argued, I argued, but we might just as well have saved ourselves the trouble. Ian was adamant. I was somewhat ironically amused when I read press articles weighing up the probability of who would earn the most – Geoff or Ian. There was no contest!

The autumn months continued in their usual frenzied way. Ian was home and our social calendar was very full. He had decided not to tour this year, being both mentally and physically tired. He had completed seven winter tours and played cricket non-stop in England for longer than that. The children were now both at school and he really hardly knew them. This was the winter he decided to step off the merry-go-round for a short while.

We had a lot of good times together. Liam would go off with Daddy on Saturday afternoon to Scunthorpe to watch the football and on Sunday we often enjoyed taking the dogs out for long walks in the woods nearby or to the coast. Ian would take the children to school in the morning and, when possible, meet them in the evening. As Christmas approached we, as proud parents, watched them both take part in their school concerts and carol services.

As ever we were still very much a source of interest to the media and in the days prior to Christmas we seemed to be inundated with journalists doing interviews for various papers or magazines and, quite often, the house would be full of television crews filming for a sports programme or a documentary. Having strange men and women walking around my house, often nine or ten at a time, with all the attendant bag and baggage of cameras and lighting was a real nuisance. I was persuaded to make one or two brief appearances myself but always preferred to keep in the background, unless it was really necessary. Mostly the crews were very pleasant, and would try hard to leave everything as they found it but, I confess, I am too house-proud and a wrongly placed chair, the overflowing ashtrays and the trails of cables irritated me. It never ceased to amaze me that it often took hours to produce a thirty-minute programme. Nowadays I know what to expect. I lay down a few rules of my own and we all work together much better.

During the weeks before Christmas, I was a little alarmed by a conversation I had with Alan Herd. A partner in his London law firm had been working on a case in conjunction with a Grimsby solicitor. During a general chit-chat the solicitor from Grimsby let it drop that he had heard on the legal grapevine that the Humberside police force were 'after Botham'. This was confirmed shortly afterwards by Vince Grimes, an ex-footballing colleague of Ian's from Scunthorpe United. He worked alongside the police in community relations and was tipped off that they were after Ian in some way. This surprised us both as we had always seemed to get along pretty well with the police locally and, in fact, Ian had done several appearances for police charities. We could only assume that the egg which stuck to their faces after the Scunthorpe assault case was still rankling them somewhat and they were trying to get their own back. It didn't particularly worry either of us, though, because we, wrongly as it turned out, assumed that, with all the fuss about drinking and driving at Christmas, that was what they would be looking out for. In fact, Ian is very strict with himself during pre-season cricket training or the football season and was, in fact, firmly 'on the wagon'. Much more worrying to Ian was, as he confided to Dad, the fact that he was sure he was being followed. They both decided not to tell me, but Ian later said that as time went on he became more and more convinced he was right about this.

We spent an unusually quiet Christmas Day, just the four of us in the morning. We watched the children open their presents and enjoyed it immensely when they played Father Christmas to us. Later in the morning, Ian drove to Thorne to bring my grandfather over for lunch. He was ninety-eight years old at the time and very sprightly. There is a wonderful rapport between the children and him: 'Tell us about when you were a little boy, Grandpa,' really does take them back into history. I drove him home shortly after tea and picked up Mrs Roy, our housekeeper from childhood days. She had been retired many years but was still regarded as very much part of the family and was an active participant in our celebrations. She had spent the day with her own sons and then came over to spend the next couple of days with us. She still thought of us as children and now Ian was included in her plan of action: 'If we all help to clear the table it will be done much quicker. Come on, Ian, you take the glasses' – and he did!

I was so pleased we had had those few days with her, as she died shortly afterwards from cancer.

New Year was to be our real family time this year. New Year's Eve found me busy in the kitchen, preparing mountains of vegetables for our 'haggis, neeps and tatties' party. It was only to be a small group: my parents, Lindsay and Paul with baby Tom and my uncle, aunt and cousins plus Grandma and Grandpa. The children were having an early tea when I heard the doorbell. Two men stood there in the darkness and I saw two more standing further down the driveway. Sensing they were policemen I feared that there had been an accident. 'I hope there's nothing wrong,' I said. 'We hope so too, Mrs Botham,' one of them remarked as they entered the house. They would say nothing more to me, just asked to speak to Ian. Memories of the horrors of the previous February engulfed me as I shepherded the children into the lounge together with Diane, pinning on my well-practised smile while telling them that some people had come to talk to Daddy on business. Two of the policemen disappeared into the other lounge with Ian. I suddenly remembered the party. I couldn't possibly have my grandparents and other relatives arriving to find police all over the house. I rang to say I wasn't feeling too well, which was perfectly true, and that I was sorry to have to put them off for the evening.

After a few moments Ian came through the kitchen. 'Did you take any of my trousers to the cleaners on Saturday?' he asked.

'Yes, a whole bundle of stuff,' I replied. 'Why?'

'They're saying there was a small packet of drugs found in the pocket.'

I couldn't believe it. 'They must be joking,' I said.

Ian turned to them. 'I have nothing to hide,' he said. 'The house is yours, search it if you want.'

'Fair enough, Mr Botham, we have a search warrant – do you wish to see it?'

'No,' was Ian's short reply. 'I've told you I've nothing to hide, go where you like.'

I remained in the kitchen with a uniformed and non-uniformed officer. They didn't caution me at all but I soon realized that among all the general chat they would throw in the odd searching question. I told them how ridiculous the whole thing was, and did they think I was going to take a pair of trousers to the cleaners knowing that they contained drugs?

During the few minutes I spent in the kitchen Lindsay and Paul arrived with Tom. They must have wondered what on earth was going on, but gamely tried to pretend nothing unusual was happening as they made their way into the lounge to join the children. Diane came through almost immediately to ask if she should stop longer or could she go, as she had been given the evening off. I asked her to check the children's bedrooms and see to their night things before she left. It wasn't until later that I realized they had never questioned her or even asked to. She walked freely about the house and then went home, having wished us a Happy New Year, which brought not much more than a wry smile from me in response.

Shortly after this Ian walked into the kitchen to say that he was going off to the police station – and did I want to go along as well? Everyone stood and waited for my reply, saying nothing. I elected to stay with the children.

Those policemen had been in our house for forty minutes. They spent half of that time talking to Ian and myself and about twenty minutes searching certain rooms in the house – our bedroom and the bathroom next to it and the guest bedroom. They didn't even go into any of the other rooms – just opened the door and had a cursory look around. The snooker room interested one of them, but only because it had lots of sporting photographs hanging on the walls.

After the exit of Ian and the police, Lindsay, Paul and I put the children to bed. It was hard to join in with the excited chattering of Liam and Sarah, and even baby Tom didn't get too many cuddles that night. We were all shaken and absolutely baffled by it all. I didn't know why Ian had gone to the police station or whether or not I should have gone with him. In fact, I didn't know where to turn, or what to do! A telephone call from Ian at about 7.30 p.m. told me that I had nothing to worry about but would I go along to the police station as there were one or two questions they wished to ask me.

Paul offered to drive me there. During that journey and the subsequent few minutes waiting at the inquiries desk we talked trivialities. Neither of us knew what to say, both of us being worried to death. It seemed right that Paul was with me at this time of trouble – he has always been solidly behind us in our more turbulent times and has often acted as a father to our children on many occasions when Ian has been away. I am sure when he married Lindsay he didn't realize that he was taking on so much responsibility, not only Lindsay, but her family as well. I am absolutely certain that he never expected to spend New Year's Eve in a police station.

When my turn at the inquiries desk arrived, I was taken through into a smaller room and allowed to have a few moments with Ian. I asked him what on earth was going on and he just repeated what he had said before at home. 'This is absolutely ridiculous,' I said. 'Don't they realize that we've been set up?' 'Don't worry about it,' was Ian's reply. 'Just go and tell them the truth.'

As I walked away I can vividly remember saying, 'I just don't believe this is happening.' A further shock awaited me when I was cautioned. This made everything suddenly become very real and frightening. Two plain clothes men, one of whom I recognized as having searched the house, questioned me. Thus began the most horrifying three hours of my life. At first they were very pleasant. Would I like a cigarette or a drink? I refused the cigarette with words the significance of which I didn't realize at the time: 'No thank you, I have never smoked,' but I did accept a welcome cup of coffee. The questions began in earnest about the trousers and the dry-cleaners. They asked me to describe exactly how I had searched the pockets. I could only say that I always searched trouser pockets for money, keys, and so on, before sending them to the cleaners and I was sure I would have done the same to this particular pair. As far as I was concerned there was nothing in them before they arrived at the dry-cleaners. Over and over again the same questions were asked in different ways. I can't remember how many times I repeated that I had never seen my husband take any drugs and to my knowledge there had never been any illegal drugs in our home; the only drugs were those prescribed for Ian's asthma and ulcer, plus any prescribed for any other member of the family.

'But there are, Mrs Botham. We have found a quantity of cannabis,' one policeman said at last. I couldn't understand any of it and said so.

The questioning went on remorselessly: 'What is your favourite drink?'

'What do you mean?'

'I mean, what drink would you like to welcome the New Year with?'

'I shan't be there to welcome the New Year.'

'We don't know that, Mrs Botham, you may be!'

At this I flared up, having kept my temper with great patience until then. 'Look! How can I convince you that I'm telling the truth?' In desperation I continued: 'I'm not a deeply religious person, but bring along the Bible and I'll swear to you on it.'

It was obvious that I was not giving them the answers they wanted me to give. I consider myself a reasonably intelligent person but the way some of the questions were framed demanded an answer that could have been taken to mean all manner of things. One of the men kept leaving the room and then returned to renew the relentless questioning. I asked to go to the ladies' room so a policewoman was brought in to accompany me. There was a New Year's Eve party going on for the families of the police. It was dreadful to be treated like a common criminal. The eyes of two little girls watched me and they giggled as I was escorted to and from the bathroom by this uniformed policewoman.

On my return the questioning was resumed and I just said: 'Look, it's obvious whatever I say you won't believe me. What can I do? Is my brother-in-law still here?' I had been there about three and a half hours so I asked that Paul should be told to go on home and I would go with Ian. 'Ah, but we don't know when Ian will be going home, Mrs Botham.' That sense of unreality again took over. Quite suddenly the questioning ceased and Paul was allowed to join me. I still wasn't allowed to go. I thought I heard an officer say: 'I suppose we could let her go on bail,' but I was quite sure I had misunderstood. To my knowledge I hadn't been arrested or charged so I couldn't possibly need bail to be released.

I still knew nothing about Ian's whereabouts but at about 11.15 I was told I could go home. Before we left, however, I was asked to fill in a form and a uniformed officer with an unemotional face and flat voice read something to me, which I didn't hear. I think now it must have been the terms of the police bail which I had graciously been allowed. I hated them all because I now realized they had thoroughly enjoyed themselves at my expense all evening and I had done nothing at all to deserve such treatment.

I asked about Ian and was told nothing. Paul and I drove home. I wonder if anyone who has not been in our position could possibly realize just how low and desperate I felt. Not only did I have the possibility of a police action to contend with, but I knew damned well that very shortly the press would headline our plight all over the world, putting their own interpretation on to it.

During the drive home Paul and I went over and over the questions I had been asked. It was still no clearer when we reached home to find Mum and Dad had arrived. They were equally shattered. While making a cup of coffee in the kitchen the saucepans of vegetables and the haggis in the fridge, all waiting to be cooked, seemed to mock me.

It was only ten minutes later when Ian arrived. I can't think why they wouldn't let us come together. They must have known that they weren't going to keep him much longer when they told me I could go. He breezed in. 'Right! What's everyone going to have then, just time to pour out before the New Year's here.' We all solemnly toasted the New Year, though there didn't seem a great deal to look forward to.

Then the talking began while the men played snooker. We were all shaken by the situation but tried to make everything as normal as possible. Ian told me what had happened to him. During the time I spent at the police station, Ian had been put into a cell alone, anxiously wondering what was happening to me. You may be asking why on earth we hadn't contacted our solicitor as, of course, we realized we should have done. Somehow doing this would have seemed to set a seal of guilt on the whole thing. We didn't need a solicitor to defend us because we thought we had done nothing that needed defending – how naive we were! I asked Ian to tell me what had happened from beginning to end and he hadn't said very much before I stopped him.

'Where did you say they found the cannabis?'

'In my top drawer.'

However, I knew that I'd only recently cleared out the chest of drawers. So we talked on until the early hours of the morning, the only certainty arising from our talks being that Alan Herd was to be contacted first thing in the morning.

He arrived post-haste to tell us what by now we knew – anyone in our position should contact a solicitor before speaking to the police. Alan spoke to us both separately; it was almost like being at the police station again except that he was much kinder and was obviously on my side. It was only after he had returned from the police station, having discovered just what the position was, that I realized I had actually been arrested on New Year's Eve and was now out on bail. This really did stun me; no longer was I on the fringe of momentous events in Ian's life, this time I was well and truly in the middle of it, and I didn't like it at all!

The *Mail*, Hull or *Daily* we are not quite sure which, quite out of the blue rang the police station for confirmation as to whether the story that Mr and Mrs Botham had been taken to the station for questioning on a drugs-related problem during New Year's Eve was true or not. The police confirmed this and that was it. Within an hour cars began to use the road outside as a parking lot and television and press cameras were busy as the telephone never stopped ringing.

Packing everything we would need for a day or two, Ian and I took shelter with my parents at Thorne while Diane took the children to Lindsay and Paul's. It was quite exciting in a morbid kind of way. Ian set off in his car to

RIGHT: Modelling in '87
Terry O'Neill
BELOW: Bunbury bunnies:
Christmas Day 1986, in
Australia. Our nanny,
Diane, is on the right
Graham Morris

The agony . . .

. . . and the ecstasy: on the charity walk from Belfast to Dublin with Ian, Liam, Sarah and Becky (Mike Gibson is between Barry McGuigan and Ian; Alex Higgins and Willie John McBride are on my left) *Graham Morris*

The Bothams come home *Graham Morris*

lead the press round the narrower lanes of Lincolnshire, successfully losing them on the way, while Dad picked me up with the luggage and drove quickly home. My parents' house is a successful hideaway because the house cannot be seen from the road. There is more than one entry and exit and we ourselves never had to answer the telephone. We watched the news bulletins and for some days found ourselves the number one issue. We kept seeing our home photographed from all angles and close-up shots of the rooms showing the Christmas tree and decorations still bravely there. The headlines were incredible: 'Drugs raid on Botham's New Year's Eve party'; 'Party Drugs Raid', etcetera. My grandparents, parents, uncle, aunt and cousins, who would have been the only guests at the party which never took place, were amazed at the descriptions of this 'wild affair'. We received dozens of telephone calls and letters of support which I still have to this day. These, plus the constant discussions with Alan and others, carried us through the next few days. Eventually we had to return home because school was about to begin its spring term. This was when I really began to worry about what effect this was all going to have on Liam and Sarah. Until now they had been carefully sheltered from television and newspapers. How much did they need to know? I told them both one evening in the bath: 'When you go back to school tomorrow you may get one or two children making fun of Mummy and Daddy. You must ignore it, tell them to go away and don't worry.' It was an early lesson in how to recognize true friendships. They asked several questions, too old not to realize that something was going on. However, I felt that when I tucked them up in bed that night they were happy. I hadn't wanted to say too much to alarm them, but enough to arm them.

I took them to school very apprehensively but was reassured to see how normally everyone reacted to us. One or two friends popped in for coffee that morning and life took on an even tenor for a few hours. As school-leaving time approached I decided to collect them myself and test the waters of opinion, although Diane usually met them. I parked the car and walked the short distance to the school gates, my heart thumping, feeling myself the focus of all eyes. Forcing myself to behave normally I walked, apparently unconcerned, towards two very good friends, Angela and Christine. The first hurdle was over. The children appeared happy as larks: Liam like 'Just William' as usual, socks round his ankles, shirt hanging out, and with grazed and filthy knees, while Sarah appeared just as she had set out, neat and tidy as ever. As we were driving home I tentatively asked whether they had had a good day at school. 'Yes, fine.' They chatted away about Christmas and all the presents they and their friends had had, then Sarah said, 'Oh, Mummy, nobody said anything nasty about you or Daddy but one of the older boys came up to me and told me that something ever so exciting had happened to you and Daddy over Christmas. You've been in gaol!' I nearly drove into the back of the next car – it sounded so funny.

It wasn't until the middle of January that we heard officially that no action would be brought against me but that Ian was to be charged with possession of 1.9 grammes of cannabis. Some of the papers had implied we were the drugs barons of the Scunthorpe area! The amount of cannabis concerned, which I am told would just about have made one cigarette, was a bit of an anti-climax.

I can't say I felt any true sense of relief that I wasn't to be charged. Because of constant media attention, I felt that my reputation had already been destroyed. In the public's mind I knew that my name would always be linked with drugs from now on. As far as Ian was concerned, 1.9 grammes of cannabis had been found in his sock drawer.

To prove that he hadn't put it there would be difficult if not impossible.

Again Ian and Alan tended to shut me out. I wanted to talk and talk about the situation because to do so made it easier for me to bear. Ian wanted to lock it away in his mind and forget about it because that was the way he always dealt with problems. I would hear him in discussion with Alan on the telephone, then when I asked what had been said his answer would be: 'Oh, nothing, everything's OK.' He would complain because practically every time he came into a room he would find me discussing it, then he would say: 'I don't want to hear about it. Alan's dealing with it and that is it!' I lost my temper frequently and our relationship began to deteriorate alarmingly.

I felt very strongly that Alan should demand a letter of apology from the police for the way they had mishandled my situation. I reasoned, I argued, but I couldn't convince them that this was the thing to do. They sympathized with my feelings and, to a great extent, agreed, but they felt it wasn't an appropriate action at that time. In hindsight I realize that their main preoccupation was to deal with the problem concerning Ian, and obviously this was right. I must have been a terrible thorn in their sides because I was totally concerned about my own reputation. Selfish, I know, but nevertheless I feel it was understandable. Even now, years later, memories of this time fill me with horror.

I stormed and raged at Ian until, never having seen me quite like that before, he left the room and asked Alan to come in to explain it all yet again, and to try to make me see reason. Alan tried hard but after about forty-five minutes he too retired defeated, loudly proclaiming that it had been worse than going fifteen rounds with Mohammed Ali.

Alan left to return to London and I walked into the lounge where Ian was stretched out on the settee. I flopped into a chair opposite him, then, suddenly, out of sheer frustration, I picked up a small glass-topped table and hurled it at him. Fortunately it missed and, moreover, it didn't break. Neither of us said anything as I stalked out and disappeared upstairs to have a bath. When I reappeared some time later Ian looked up at me and said, 'Feeling better now?'

For several months now we had suspected that our telephone was being tapped and I had reported our suspicions both to the post office and to the police. I was amazed to discover that neither service was unduly surprised by this and treated our complaints quite seriously. For this reason we used our telephone as little as possible and, for anything important, would pop over to friends' houses. When in the mood Ian would ring up someone from our own telephone who knew about the tapping and make outrageous statements for the benefit of anyone else who might be listening.

It occurred to me that Ian's parents really hadn't been kept very well informed about all that was going on, so we arranged a meeting at Lindsay's which is a good halfway house between their home in Yeovil and ours in Epworth. They were, as expected, terribly worried about the whole thing and upset because we hadn't been able to explain everything as it was happening. Ian's sister, Wendy, with her husband Paul had also joined us. In spite of the reason for the meeting it turned into a happy family get-together. You could say it became the party we had missed on New Year's Eve.

It had been arranged that Ian's mother would travel back with us for a few days. On the way home, as a treat for the children we stopped at the 'Happy Eater' restaurant on the A38 near Derby. It was the first time Ian and myself had been anywhere in public since the 1st of January. To see and hear the response of the other customers to us was heart-warming. Many came over to wish us luck and to assure us that all was well as far as they were concerned.

Of all days the court hearing was to be 14 February. Ian has always made much of Valentine's Day, never missing it. Even from far-flung corners of the world a dozen red roses have always appeared with an appropriate message. This year I stonily told him that I didn't want any; it didn't seem fitting on such a trying day. In fact I was very upset when no roses were forthcoming! I was so against everything which had gone on that I was now becoming very anti-Ian. He was, as usual, coping admirably, even with my unpredictable behaviour, convinced with his typical Saggitarian optimism that everything would be all right in the end. In the circumstances he had decided he had no choice but to plead guilty.

It didn't matter that possession of 1.9 grammes of cannabis is classed, rightly or wrongly, by many people as a minor misdemeanour. I didn't care that there were thousands of similar convictions up and down the country. It was no consolation to me that many people told me it was such a trivial thing it wasn't worth worrying about. I knew the widespread repercussions that might – no, would – follow. I wasn't wrong. Nowadays, whenever Ian appears or is mentioned on any programme the subject of drugs is almost always brought into the conversation. On some chat shows we have both been subjected to question after question concerning drug abuse. When it is mentioned, no one says 'convicted of possessing 1.9 grammes of cannabis, approximately one-thirteenth of an ounce.' They state boldly: 'Ian Botham, who was in 1985 convicted on a drugs charge.' It could have been ten tons of heroin as far as they are concerned. To me, who utterly condemns drugs misuse of any kind, the whole affair was both stupid and mortifying.

Although I wanted no more to do with any of it, my

instinctive feelings of loyalty and love made me accompany
Ian and Alan to the courtroom at Scunthorpe.

On arrival we were greeted by one of the policemen
who had interrogated me. 'Hello, Kathy,' he said blithely.
'How are you?'

'Mrs Botham to you,' I replied. I just couldn't forget my
recent treatment.

'Steady, Kathryn,' Alan warned, but I took no heed. I
felt nothing but contempt for all of them at that time. Even
my inbuilt politeness deserted me and I just held my head
high, ignoring them all.

I couldn't believe the number of press and television
reporters who were there. During the recess I was told by
an acquaintance, who also happened to be a policeman,
that several officers felt we should be allowed to slip away
afterwards through a side door. It was no surprise to me
that this suggestion fell on deaf ears. The officer in charge
decreed that we were to be given no privileges and should
be treated as everyone else would be. Does everyone else
have the world's press around when leaving Scunthorpe
Magistrates' Court? We ran the gamut of them all and
drove off after Ian received his £100 fine. My fury was not
assuaged when I learned that, in the police notes about the
case given to the magistrates to consider, it was clearly
stated that Mr Botham had refused to allow a search of his
house until a search warrant had been procured.

When I arrived home to be greeted by the children – but
no Valentine flowers – a degree of sanity returned. Ian was
not with me, he had gone straight to football training
where he was able to work off his displeasure. When he
eventually came home he didn't want to talk about the
affair at all. As far as he was concerned that was it, finished.
Walking straight through the kitchen door he picked up
the telephone and arranged a holiday for us all.

For a few days we were able to get away from it all. It

was only after we escaped that we realized just how much pressure there had been. Just the four of us enjoyed being alone together, if you know what I mean. Relaxing in lovely surroundings, walking or driving as the mood took us, exploring the countryside with our children; gradually the turmoil ebbed and we found a new sense of peace.

Over previous weeks Ian and I had become almost total strangers. During all our married life our two very opposite natures had drawn us close together, each finding strengths in the other which we lacked in ourselves. We had had strong disagreements in the past but we had always been able to recognize and appreciate each other's point of view, even if we didn't agree with it. We had begun to find no point of agreement and no ease of reconciliation. We had argued disproportionately over all sorts of things both minor and major, unable to find any common ground.

During this short break we were able to find each other again and by the time we came home we had sorted out many things and made some very important decisions. It was then we made up our minds to move. I no longer felt at ease in the house. It had been featured on the world's television, neighbours had told us of snoopers wandering round the house and gardens, and cameras had photographed it through windows and from all angles. Very importantly, Liam, now seven, was having problems with older boys at school who were jibing him unmercifully about Ian.

Generally, however, we had received tremendous support from everyone and most of our worst fears had proved groundless. The thing we had lost most sleep about was how the TCCB would view the recent events. In fact they issued a statement which made it clear that Ian would be allowed to be considered for selection in the future but that from 1985 any cricketer 'found guilty of possessing or using illegal drugs which bring the game into disrepute' would be penalized severely. This was a great relief to us all but we also received some nasty knocks. Just before Christmas a company called Wiggins Teape had agreed, in principle, a lucrative deal with Ian, who was to be used in a promotions campaign for stationery. They had originally been very enthusiastic, now they withdrew saying that they feared the recent publicity might damage their image. I believe Wiggins Teape is a subsidiary of a tobacco company!

David Gower replaced Ian, jolly good for David. We are both very fond of him, but whenever I saw his face smiling at me from the Wiggins Teape adverts, which appeared everywhere that summer, I felt sad and irritated.

We also received a letter from Saab UK Ltd who had sponsored Ian for several years. They regretted they would have to ask Ian to return the car they had loaned him as part of the sponsorship deal. They had decided, we were informed, to use other forms of publicity. It wasn't just the financial aspect which hurt; much more than that it was the loss of faith in Ian. The hierarchy at Saab assured us that their decision to ditch Ian was nothing at all to do with recent events, but the date on their letter was 19 January, the very day the press told the world that Ian Botham was to be charged with possessing pot. We had no way of knowing how many people would no longer want Ian to work for them. Two main sponsors, Nike and Duncan Fearnley, had contacted us immediately on learning of our trouble, offering us help and support and I blessed them for this.

However, the future was uncertain, the telephone didn't ring as often and the mail brought hundreds of letters of support but not enough requests for appearances. The stage was set for the appearance of Tim and Maxi Hudson.

— 11 —

The Hudson Affair and the Big Walk

During Ian's benefit season Tim Hudson had arranged a Botham/Boycott match at his home in Birtles, Cheshire. Following a telephone call from him in America late one Sunday evening, we arranged to meet him and Maxi at their home, immediately following our Lake District holiday at Easter 1985. We drove from the Lakes to this beautiful old hall near Macclesfield and were welcomed by them in the driveway. Ian walked in saying, 'We ought to have a bottle of champagne, we have something to celebrate.' He told them that our third child was due to arrive the following November. As I had spent much of the Easter holiday in bed because I felt so wretched and sick, Ian felt the need to explain why I might be making a few quick exits from our discussions. This piece of information was greeted less than enthusiastically and the subject was quickly changed. Despite this, Tim and Maxi made us feel very welcome, and for a couple who had recently felt the depths of despair their observations and promises opened the door at the end of what had been a long dark tunnel. Much of what they said made sense to us. 'Ian,' said Tim, 'should make a fortune. He hasn't been promoted as he should have been. I shall help him make that fortune.' He was as extravagant in his speech as he was in his clothes and pony-tail hairstyle. A cricket enthusiast, his home was full of cricket memorabilia. I was interested to see that each chair in the dining room had a cricket blazer or sweater draped over the back, obviously collected over a period of time.

At this time no mention was made of Tim becoming Ian's manager. He was, he said, interested in helping to promote Ian. Tim's image of Ian was that of a true English gentleman, big and strong, an English lion with charisma to boot. We left Birtles feeling happy; the future appeared to hold a lot for us.

True to his word, Tim worked fast and furiously and a period of intense activity began for us all. We had several more meetings, travelling all over the country to fit in with the cricket fixture list. Gradually the concept of a range of clothing emerged, to be marketed under the tradename of 'Hudson's Hardware by choice Botham' and aimed at the British and American market. It was to be in the style of pre-war England, when gentlemen were gentlemen and croquet on the lawn was the 'in' thing. Blazers and cricket flannels of the highest quality were designed and hats were to be popularized. Certainly Tim got things done – yesterday if he so decreed – and the whole idea gained momentum. Ian was literally the clothes-peg on which all this was hung but I had reservations. To be honest, I occasionally felt slightly embarrassed by some of the things Ian had to wear. He carried it off with his usual aplomb and, as the majority of people around were enthusiastic, I kept my opinions to myself.

Ian was busy playing cricket and occupied with his various commitments, whereas I was busy making arrangements to move house. Following the police raid on our home at Epworth and all its consequences we had decided to move. We were sorry to leave the people of Epworth behind, having had some very happy times there and making many friends, but I no longer felt happy in my own home. The police search at New Year had violated it for me. In addition, we felt it was time to change the children's school and, not wanting them to board, we had to move to do this. Much to everyone's surprise and, contrary to the rumours about houses in Somerset, as far as Ian was concerned it was the further north the better. As I have always loved north Yorkshire we had no trouble in deciding on an area around the Dales or the North Yorkshire moors, and were fortunate to find exactly what we wanted almost immediately.

Once it was discovered where we were to live, the people of the tiny village were inundated with newsmen asking their opinion of their new neighbours. With typical Yorkshire forthrightness the press were told to clear off and leave us alone. They would make up their minds about us when they met us. Happily the move proved to be just the right thing: we thoroughly enjoy living in the area, have made a lot of new friends, but are still near enough to see the old ones frequently. The change of school has also been a great success, and Liam and Sarah like it enormously, joining in numerous activities with typical Botham vigour.

As Ian became more and more involved with Tim, it became increasingly evident that the hoped-for liaison between Tim and Reg Hayter, who had been Ian's agent since his career began, would not happen, and Reg decided it was time for him to retire from the scene. There were regrets on all sides; that is, from Reg's side and our side.

Tim and Maxi now really came into their own. I was reassured to see so many cricketing personalities with obvious faith in Tim. He had his own cricket ground at Birtles and planned cricketing festivals, running his own team 'The Hudson Hollywood Eleven', with Brian Close as captain, and he certainly appeared to know all the right people. I saw no objection when it was suggested that he should become Ian's agent. I was certainly not prepared for the attempted takeover which followed.

On the eve of the Australia v. Somerset match it was decided to hold a press launch to announce their partnership. From the sidelines I found the whole thing farcical. It had been arranged to satisfy the inquisitive nature of the press but it had been done too quickly and there was little to show and even less to say. I sat there feeling uncomfortable and wondering what other people were making of it. I learned then that Tim was very good at waffling; he spoke for a very long time about absolutely nothing except his admiration for Ian. I don't think the media were too impressed either, and for once I agreed with them. However, at the end the main participants seemed well satisfied so I kept my counsel.

As the season progressed I became increasingly irritated by the constant presence of Tim and Maxi everywhere we went. They expected and were given tickets for every day of every match, which left even fewer to be divided among family and friends. The Hudsons took it for granted that they would be welcome everywhere. Test match cricket has rules and regulations and there are inner sanctums at every ground where admittance is strictly limited by invitation only. This includes a pleasant lunch which is an opportunity for wives and other relatives and close friends to meet each other. Each player is allocated two tickets and they are often pooled and redistributed as needed. This season I found myself in some awkward situations as for this, too, Tim and Maxi expected to be the first in line. I found myself drinking coffee out of a cardboard cup and eating a sandwich while the Hudsons joined the other wives for lunch.

I decided not to make an issue out of it. I don't think Ian realized quite what was happening but I hated it when organizers would quietly take me on one side and say, 'I realize, Mrs Botham, that Ian wants his agent with him but we really haven't the room for everyone.' I would have had about as much success in stopping them from going where they wanted as a mini trying to stop a steamroller, so my answer would be quite open and frank, 'I'm sorry. There's really nothing I can do about that, but do have a word with them about it.' They didn't, of course, so it was invariably a case of 'and Tim and Maxi came too'.

To a certain extent I could cope with all this, but what I really couldn't take was the excessive adulation which Tim showered on Ian. Ian would stand by his side and listen as Tim uttered glowing words of praise to all who would listen. Ian Botham could conquer the world, he was saying in effect. There was nobody like him; he could do any-thing; the world was his oyster. I do believe that at this time Ian began to believe it himself, which made living with him extremely difficult. The Hudsons monopolized Ian and he spent all his free time travelling up the M6 towards Birtles instead of the A1 towards his new home, into which we had moved at the beginning of August, while Ian was playing in a Test match at Old Trafford. A room was put at his disposal at Birtles and they exhorted him to stay there at every opportunity.

Liam had spent much of his school summer holiday with Ian. When Ian was at Birtles I was invited along too but I went very rarely as I felt uncomfortable and Ian and I would invariably end up rowing. My pregnancy gave me the excuse I needed for not doing too much travelling, so I became an onlooker in the Botham-Hudson saga rather than a participant. They always say the onlooker sees most of the game.

Some readers may consider that I was weak-willed, but over the years I have learned how to handle Ian, and constantly being around and nagging is not the way. I state my point of view very clearly and then leave him alone to digest it. I stated my view of recent events and the way it was affecting us all in no uncertain terms, and then stayed at home for him to think it all over. This mode of attack usually works but in this case I was not so confident. Ian was so determined to make the Hudson-Botham team work.

As always the winter touring side was announced in September. The 1986 tour was to be to the West Indies but not until after Christmas, and Ian was in the squad. This gave us October, November and December together. Some years earlier Ian had become interested in leukaemia research. He had visited a hospital in Taunton and had been asked to have a word with some of the young boys in one of the wards. They seemed so well when he spoke to them that he couldn't believe that within a year they might well be dead from the disease. For some time we had kept in touch with that hospital and we set up a fund which had a float to help relatives with the expenses of visiting their children in hospital. Whenever he was asked, Ian visited children suffering from this dreadful disease. 'It isn't enough though,' he would say, 'I'd like to do something that will give them a chance of living.' During one of our long walks in the Lake District one Easter he turned to me and said, 'That's it. When I have time I'll walk from John O' Groats to Land's End and hope for sponsorship and donations for the Leukaemia Research Association.' I knew he would do it. This year, 1985, was the first opportunity he had had to put his plan into operation.

Tim and Maxi Hudson were not at all impressed by this. It was to take five weeks of Ian's possible earning time and they stated that had Tim been representing Ian at the time the walk was arranged they would not have allowed him to do it. It was Ian's turn to be unimpressed; nothing short of physical injury would stop him, and I think it was at about this time that Ian began to wonder about his links with Tim, although he said nothing then. I had gone through my own period of being unimpressed when I first realized that I was pregnant and that the baby would arrive right in the middle of the walk. I was delighted about the baby, but I did wish I could pick a time when Ian would be around. So many people expected Ian to abandon the idea when he learned about the baby but I knew he wouldn't and didn't expect or want him to. I knew he couldn't take days off because the whole expedition had already been most carefully planned, but I did demur quietly when he suggested that it would be difficult to get to Doncaster to see me and the new arrival immediately. Typical dedication to duty carried a little too far, I pointed out. He obviously thought it over and duly arrived on the evening of Becky's birth.

We spent a happy October holiday at the log cabin in Scotland, marred only by a stupid press story about how Ian had shot a pet stag, 'Old Sid'. I believe Old Sid is still alive and well to this day. We were also somewhat embarrassed by a 'Breakfast Time' television team who arrived in accordance with an arrangement which no one had told me about. We thought they were newspaper reporters hassling us about Old Sid so we drew the curtains of our log cabin and kept well away. Once we realized who they were we invited them in for coffee and made them feel more welcome!

Friday 25 October found us on our way to John O' Groats ready to start Ian's long trek south. The closer we got, the realization that the next day would see him retracing the journey on foot dawned on Ian, and he became quieter and quieter. He tried to work out whether the hills we were now traversing easily in the car would be part of the first or second day's walk.

The beginning of the walk was well heralded by journalists and television crews. I think that many of them had planned to cover the first day and possibly the last, but as the walk progressed and caught the public imagination, the whole thing engendered enormous publicity. BBC's 'Breakfast Time' made a quick decision to cover every day and it took off from then onwards.

With millions of others I watched each morning and saw Ian cheerfully marching onwards, jollying others along with him. Rather like the Pied Piper his entourage grew and grew. Each day would bring more walkers and more collections and many people were carried along in the exuberance of it all. I often wondered how he kept going. He rang me each evening, always sounding thoroughly exhausted. He tried to describe the atmosphere to me, the welcome they received from every town and village and the generosity of the people. It was difficult for anyone not there to understand, and I would so much like to have been there with him. On the Sunday before Becky was born they crossed from Scotland and finished that day at Penrith. We had had the first snow falls of winter and, determined to meet Ian at the walk, I joined the group about seven miles north of Penrith. Liam had set out early that morning with his mini rugby colleagues to walk with his Daddy from Carlisle.

We parked the car in a layby high up north of Penrith and looked towards Scotland seeing the lovely snow-capped mountains and the bleak moorland bare on this winter's day. Far in the distance over the winding roads we saw the hazard lights of the first car, then we heard the music we had heard each morning on television and, streaming behind, the enthusiastic band of walkers, helpers and collectors swept along in the slipstream of determination. I will never forget the feeling of pride I had when I saw it all. The courage of many was obvious as they limped along on sore, aching feet and legs. Men and women, some striding out, others trudging along but all united in a common cause. The children amazed me; hopping, running, dancing along, stopping everyone, cars included, and shaking collecting boxes, inviting – no, ordering – everyone they met to contribute.

I hadn't intended to do any walking but an irresistible urge to join the throng overtook me and, getting out of the car, I joined Ian. The pace of the walk surprised me. I was swept into it as if into a jet stream. I felt as if I could have gone the whole way but, mindful of the seven long miles still to come, Ian insisted that I should go back to the car and join him later. This I did just outside Penrith and walked through the town with him. People crushed round us, members of the backup team appeared to protect us from the pushes and accidental kicks of people jostling each other to shake Ian's hand or personally hand over money or just to wish him luck. I walked on in silence, realizing that conversation would have been useless as Ian was talking to himself, telling his legs to keep moving. At the finishing point for the day there were crowds in the carpark, each person bent on obtaining an autograph. We walked straight through to the mobile home which was to take us to the hotel. I was saddened to hear one or two people complaining bitterly that he hadn't stopped to sign the pieces of paper they were pushing under his nose. If only they had realized what a state he was in at the time I'm sure they wouldn't have complained.

Ian has always been happy to sign autographs but has strict rules about it: either all or none. If he hasn't the time to oblige everyone who is asking, then he refuses to be selective. In this case he couldn't have signed one, let alone all. He was whipped away and wrapped in blankets, and sat like a zombie mentally and physically exhausted. I had joined him at the worst possible time; he was at a very low ebb, his mind hurting as much as his aching body and sore feet. Jimmy Saville had contacted him prior to the walk to warn him that the mental fatigue was far worse than any physical discomfort. This was Ian's 'slough of despond' where, I think, his body was telling his mind that it couldn't take any more.

The original idea had been that Ian was to be the only one walking all the way. Three others – Chris Lander, then a journalist with the *Daily Mirror*; Phil Rance, a businessman from Manchester whose father had died of leukaemia; and John Border, brother of Alan, the Australian cricket captain – had joined him in this intention. They became known as 'Prisoners of the Walk' (POWs) and each had his peaks and troughs, luckily at different times so that the fit ones were able to carry the other along with them, in turns cajoling, using sarcasm and threats.

Still zombie-like at the hotel, Ian limped stiffly towards his room and sought the relief of a steaming bath. At this point he was sixteen days and roughly three hundred miles into his journey. He had blistered feet, aching knees and sore shins. None of these worried him or me. What did cause me anxiety was his exhaustion, which was so unusual in him. He lay on his bed, which Andy had propped at an angle, to alleviate swollen knees and ankles, and ordered his first meal of the day which, when it arrived, he was too tired to eat.

I had intended to stay an hour or two with him as, with the baby's impending arrival, I didn't know when I would be able to see him again. Dad had been walking beside Ian that day and he and Mum had taken the children to eat in the hotel restaurant. I joined them, realizing that there was no way Ian would get out of bed, let alone spend an hour or two with us, to suggest an earlier than arranged journey home. Crossing the hotel foyer I came up behind a group of smartly dressed people who were agitated about something. 'Who does he think he is?' I heard one say. 'Who is he to say he can't come to our function tonight? We've had it arranged for weeks.' I walked on and found the walk organizer sitting with the family. 'What's going on, Steve?' I asked. 'Someone's upset about something.' I learned that the local leukaemia association had raised money for the fund and someone had told them that Ian would receive the cheque personally. Ian, in fact, knew nothing about it and in any event would have been unable to attend, so I offered to take his place. This pleased the organizers though there were rumblings of displeasure in certain quarters. I would like to have told the grumblers just what a strain it was to keep going: twenty-five to thirty miles a day, and the next day, and the next . . . and have invited them to join in, not just for a day but for at least a week. I believe I am correct in saying that it was the first time the walk down Britain has been attempted in such a short, specified time.

The following Wednesday, in the early hours of the morning, Rebecca Kate Botham made her appearance. She was born at 3.10 a.m. Careful arrangements had been made to inform Ian, involving radio telephones, etcetera, but at this time in the morning I decided that there was no point in waking him. There was nothing he could do and a particularly long stretch was in front of him that day. I detailed my mother to ring him not earlier than 6.30 a.m. when I knew he would have to be getting up to make the careful preparation needed for an 8.30 start. I understand he ran down the corridor shouting the news to everyone, and that day's walk was a particularly happy one as the news spread. Becky was a lovely baby and I was a lucky Mum, as a generous supply of flowers and toys and clothes for the new baby came flooding in. The news was broken on 'Breakfast Television' before we had a chance to ring around the family. In a link-up with Ian, Selina Scott asked Ian what was to be the new baby's name. We hadn't then decided so he remarked, 'Perhaps we'll call her after you,

Selina.' This explains why she has several gifts with the name 'Selina' on them. She will keep these to remind her of the circumstances of her birth.

Becky's arrival was timed extremely well, because she arrived when Ian was the nearest he was ever to be to Doncaster Royal Infirmary where all our children had been born. The BBC had tried to arrange a helicopter to fly Ian over as soon as the day's walk finished, but hadn't managed it. Instead they hired an old white Daimler, a beautiful old car which travelled only at a stately 50 mph. Ian hadn't been able to set off before the massage and foot treatment he needed to enable him to carry on the next day, so it was almost 10 p.m. when he arrived, trailing the inevitable posse of television cameras. Liam and Sarah had been allowed to stay behind to meet Daddy so it became a happy family reunion. Both Ian and I were absolutely shattered, but we smiled obligingly for the cameras and said all the mundane things that were expected of us. It obviously disrupted the routine of the hospital but the staff were most helpful and the other patients very interested in what was going on.

You would think that after all the time it takes to produce a baby we would have had the name chosen, but we just couldn't agree on one and had decided to wait, hoping that a name would spring to mind after the birth. So after the television crews had disappeared we set about solving this weighty problem. After some rather startling suggestions from the children, Liam and Sarah very reluctantly went home to bed. They had been eagerly awaiting a new brother or sister and now the moment had arrived it was all rather dream-like to them. I looked forward to a cosy chat with the husband I hadn't really chatted with for weeks. He climbed on to the bed, stretched out and said, 'Now, how are you feeling, Tink?' and promptly went to sleep.

I was delighted when the specialist told me that I could go home the next morning. Ian, of course, was still wending his way down England so Mum came immediately to collect me and baby Becky. I had only known myself for an hour that I was coming out that day, so I was amazed to see such a collection of reporters and cameramen waiting for me. I was not amazed but amused to see the way in which the Sister, who had come to see me off, dealt with the cameraman who wanted me to stroll across the carpark on a freezing November day with a day-and-a-half-old baby in my arms.

For weeks I had been hoping against hope that the baby would be early and she was by two days, so I was able to carry out my plan to meet Ian as a surprise on the Kidderminster to Ombersley stretch of the walk. Lindsay and Paul and young Tom live at Crossway Green, a village between these two points. I was able to stay at Lindsay's house with five-day-old Becky then, just as the walkers arrived at the top of the road, I appeared before a startled Ian with Becky in my arms, and joined him just for a few yards. He was totally surprised, giving me a quick kiss and not stopping in his long strides. He swept Becky into his arms and she was carried along for a while. A photographer friend who was covering the walk hadn't realized it was me and was somewhat confused by the sight of a young woman with an obviously very young baby leaping into the centre of the mêlée.

I returned to the warmth and shelter of Lindsay's home, having quickly arranged to meet Ian later at his hotel. Paul had walked that day with Ian and now their son, two-year-old Tom, was wheeled along in his pushchair by Uncle Ian whom he clearly adores. I don't think he travelled so quickly in his chair either before or since. He clung on grimly as the yards flicked by, enjoying every minute of it.

This time when meeting after a day's walking, Ian was much better both mentally and physically. In fact, this time Chris Lander was the one who was 'down'. After completing the day's stint Ian had driven back up the road to find him struggling badly over the last few miles. He handed him a bottle of whisky and said, 'Come on, Chris, you can do it,' and drove slowly alongside the exhausted walker, talking him home. A few swigs of the bottle poured new strength into him and he made it.

Just under a fortnight later the walk was due to finish at Land's End and we planned a full-scale family reunion. I hadn't really been able to become a part of it all and I don't think anyone who wasn't there the whole time can realize how much the whole project meant to the people closely involved with it. It was an emotional ending and I remember thinking, 'How on earth is he going to be able to come down to earth after all this?' The walk was immensely successful financially but, more than that, the Leukaemia Research Association were delighted by the way Ian had put them on the map. People all over Britain now know about them.

Within four days of the conclusion of the walk, Ian was in America at the behest of Tim Hudson. To this day, I don't know why he went. Nothing seemed to be achieved except that, once more, he was away from us all. Arriving home just two days before Christmas, it was very obvious that Ian was finding it difficult to adapt to life at home. It was a fraught time for me. Ian had declared our home an open house for John Border, who took him literally, and these two, together with Andy, made three men around the place for me to cater for.

Just before Ian went on the West Indies tour, Harry Greenway, MP arranged a tea at the Houses of Parliament in honour of the leukaemia walk, at which Mrs Thatcher had agreed to be present. We were all thrilled about this and duly turned up to be greeted by an old friend, Jeffrey Archer. We were taken into the nether regions of the Houses of Parliament where a splendid tea had been prepared. I was pleased because I felt that, for once, Ian was getting recognition from high places. He has always had the public's regard, but I have always felt that the establishment has ignored his achievements, cricketing or otherwise. This occasion was to prove no different. The Westland affair had blown up and Mrs Thatcher found it impossible to leave the Commons even for a moment. She did take the time to scribble a note to Mr Greenway, expressing her regrets. Ian is a fan of Mrs Thatcher's. I know he doesn't agree with me, but I was bitterly disappointed for him and felt that the time spent writing a letter to say she couldn't come would have been better spent telling us personally. I have never been particularly interested in politics, but on the one occasion I have met her at a reception at Number 10 I was greatly impressed by her as a person. She made us feel very welcome. Perhaps I felt she was something of a kindred spirit as I know how disturbed she must have been by the wild stories which have abounded about her family.

Ian began the fateful tour of the West Indies and I settled down to a few weeks of comparative peace before flying to Antigua at the end, for a fortnight's holiday. My fears about the relationship between Ian and Tim and Maxi Hudson now began to be realized. The first 'event' of that eventful tour was a report in the *Today* newspaper on 19 March claiming that drugs had been linked with the leukaemia walk, and that information had been handed to the police from a 'press source'. The press source subsequently turned out to be Simon Worthington who was working for a national paper but who had joined the walk on the pretence of working for a health and fitness magazine. In the event the police, having taken a number of statements from people on the walk, took no action.

A few days later, during our Easter holiday in the Lake District, worse was to come. Tim Hudson, the agent who, in his own words, was 'to put Ian on top of the world', was actually quoted on the front page of the *Star* news-paper as having said, 'Of course Ian smokes cannabis. Doesn't everyone?' When asked to explain this he denied having given an interview and claimed that he was tricked into a statement which he had never really meant. I shall never understand it. The whole thing was so illogical.

Alan Herd and I had already had a long talk over Easter and he too shared the feelings I had had for a long time. I had sensed that as far as Tim and Maxi were concerned the children and I had no place in Ian's life. They had great plans for him not only here in Britain but in America as well and to put this plan into operation I am sure they wanted Ian Botham with no family ties. I rang Ian in the West Indies and told him everything I felt about them. His faith was beginning to waver and, although unconvinced that Tim had said anything at all about drugs, he in turn had a long talk with Alan. As he is wont to do, Ian made his mind up very quickly and instructed Alan to sever all ties with the Hudsons as quickly as possible.

There had been good times during Tim and Ian's asso-ciations and he had been very kind and complimentary about the children. Liam especially had always been made welcome when he had visited Birtles with his father.

During the Hudson-Botham liaison the National Por-trait Gallery had invited Ian to have his portrait painted for inclusion in their collection. This is an honour and, I believe, Ian was the only cricketer so honoured since W. G. Grace. When the portrait by John Bellany was completed there was an official unveiling at the National Portrait Gallery. Ian was on tour and so couldn't attend, but I took the children along. I didn't like Ian's portrait, and Liam and Sarah didn't know what to make of it. They were standing in front of it, gazing upwards, when a friend stopped behind them. 'What do you think of Daddy's portrait?' she asked. 'I think it's bloomin' awful.'

'Aunty Chris!' exclaimed a shocked Liam. 'You mustn't say that. Mummy says if anyone asks I should say that it's very interesting!'

With the exclusion of Tim Hudson from our lives, home became an even busier place as all the work previously done by him now came to me. I now found the duties of secretary/agent added to my various jobs of mother, nurse, wife, confidante, but, as Ian will tell you, I thrive on being busy and for a while I didn't mind a bit.

12

Into the Limelight

At the end of the infamous tour of Barbados in 1986 we did manage to find a hideaway where we enjoyed five days of relative peace. It wasn't an easy time. We found it difficult to forget the past week or two and, both possessing short fuses at that time, found we had to tread very carefully in our relationship with each other. The *News of the World* hadn't finished with us either. A woman known to the cricketing fraternity as 'Zany Zelda' had been persuaded to reveal all! I didn't even bother to read her story. 'Zelda', whose real name is Vivienne, had travelled around with her husband Steve Whiting, ex-cricket reporter on the *Sun* newspaper, for several years. During this time she had caused much embarrassment to her husband's colleagues, as well as to members of the various touring parties. She was also a self-confessed drug addict as even the *News of the World* admitted. I didn't want to lower myself to read what 'Zelda' had to say and was content just to get a summary from Alan Herd who telephoned us from England.

The day following Zelda's 'revelations', Ian and I had the most idyllic time on Green Island, a smaller island about twenty-five minutes away from Antigua by speedboat. We swam, sunbathed, Ian learned to scuba-dive and we hunted for shells to take back to the children. Wandering hand in hand along the beach we noticed a small dinghy approaching. Out of it stepped a man who immediately introduced himself to Ian. 'The two B's, castaways on a desert island.' It was Alan Bristow of Bristows helicopters. The Westland affair had just been making headline news over the world. How strange that he and Ian should meet by chance at this time in the middle of nowhere!

Those five days had done us a great deal of good. In an odd twist of life these dark days are, I believe, good for the soul and good for a marriage. At first the dreadful times the press had put us through pulled us apart; eventually, however, we became closer than ever. It was as if the tensions which had stretched us taut held fast at the ultimate point, then sprang us back together again. In our searchings for a way through all the pressures we were able to analyse our lives together, bringing to the fore what we didn't like about each other, talking freely about anything and everything. We swept the cupboards of our minds free of doubts and dislikes, ready to start again in a way that few people have the chance to do.

On our return from these few precious days together we were met by the children and travelled straight down to Somerset as the English cricket season was about to begin. Alan Herd had also arrived to discuss some important steps in Ian's libel action against the *Mail on Sunday*, although I wasn't to realize just how important it would turn out to be. The *Mail on Sunday*, of course, had been the paper which published allegations that Ian and other England cricketers (whom they didn't name) had smoked 'pot' on tour in New Zealand.

I well remember sitting in a café in Taunton with Ian and Alan. It was chaotic. Ian was dashing around all day – among other things to get his hair cut. The children were with us, wanting to go here, there and everywhere, not

having been to Taunton for ages. Concentration was at a
premium. I felt in a turmoil, knowing that somehow or
other we all had to speak about something vital, but not
knowing how this could be done without creating a sense
of abnormality with Liam and Sarah. A peculiar feeling
arose that I was on one planet dealing with one life, and
simultaneously on a different planet dealing with another
life. Eventually, Ian, Alan and myself were able to find a
few minutes to talk privately in this Taunton café, with
buns and coffee, to discuss a momentous decision. I even
remember Alan's colleague Neil queueing up to get the
coffee and buns.

Nobody seemed to know what to say, though I began
to sense that something I didn't want to hear was coming.
It duly arrived. Alan said he felt we, and he stressed the
word 'we', had to get rid of Ian's action against the *Mail
on Sunday*. He explained what legal actions could cost –
win or lose – and that nothing was certain in life, and so
on. He explained that a legal action of that substance
would take weeks to be heard, that the whole of the
cricketing establishment would be under the microscope,
that many cricketers would be involved in giving evidence
and so on. I could not have cared less, not being at all
impressed by these arguments. The only point he made
that struck a sympathetic chord was the effect that a full-
length trial in the full glare of the media would have on
our family life – win or lose. After all those months of
living with this thing I could only feel total despair: despair
at having to go along with a decision I felt was being made
for me. Yet again, it was Ian's decision and yet again I was
the other person most closely affected. We didn't need to
discuss for long; instinct told us Alan's suggestion was the
right one for our peace of mind, though my mind was not
too peaceful at that precise moment.

Alan was asked to sort out an end to the action in

discussion with the *Mail on Sunday*'s lawyers. Ian agreed to write something in the paper about the pressures of his life and of some occasion when he *had* smoked pot. I agreed to write an article giving my views about what Ian was saying. I might add at this stage that I do not agree that cannabis should be legalized and I strongly disapprove of its use.

In any event, it is interesting to observe that although Ian has to scrutinize carefully the prescribed drugs he takes for his asthma and stomach ulcer, cannabis is not on the TCCB list of prohibited drugs. They had decreed in 1985 that any cricketer found to be misusing drugs in the future would be severely dealt with. To admit to smoking pot on occasions before that would be like trying someone for not wearing seat belts in 1965 when the law was only introduced in 1983 – or so we thought. So, after discussion with Alan Herd as to its wording, we decided to go ahead and the fateful article was duly written and printed. We felt good, the slate wiped clean, no libel action hanging over our heads, no more legal fees to pay. Unpleasantness was behind us – or so we thought. We set off to Lindsay and Paul's home near Worcester to meet Mum and Dad so that as a family we could celebrate Dad's birthday, with a lunch on board the Severn Valley Steam Railway on the following day, a Sunday.

Sitting watching the television that Saturday evening while the men had gone off together for a drink, we turned over to see the news. The headlines were the more startling for being totally unexpected: 'Ian Botham has put his Test future in jeopardy by admitting to drug-taking in the past.' 'Oh my goodness,' I thought. 'It's all going to go wrong.'

And go wrong it did, with a vengeance. Again all the newspapers were rife with speculation as to Ian's future game. I travelled back with him to Brighton where Somerset were playing Sussex to hear that he had been suspended from playing in the Texaco Trophy one-day matches pending a decision from Lord's. I hadn't expected anything like this; not allowing him to play was surely hanging him before he was found guilty. I felt then that the TCCB were bowing to media pressure and that some of its members were pleased to have found something that enabled them to try to finish Ian as far as playing for England was concerned.

While Ian was tied up answering questions from the media and taking telephone calls galore from Alan, I was escorted into the physio's room at Brighton. I had baby Becky with me; she was finding the constant attention of the press frightening, so we had to find a shelter away from them. One after another the players, both from Somerset and Sussex, came to see me with words of support for Ian and condemnation of the authorities. I particularly remember Viv Richards being immensely supportive. He was helping both Ian and me by taking Ian's role of getting me through a difficult situation. Knowing Ian so well, he realized that Ian's way was simply to tell me not to worry, which would have been pointless in these circumstances. 'Have faith,' said Viv. 'I know, Kath, that nothing but good will eventually come out of this, however black it looks today.'

Whenever Ian has had bad times in his career, Viv Richards has always been there to support him. While not always agreeing with him, he has the knack of being able to guide Ian, steering him back on to the right tracks. When people are under such immense pressure they do tend to fly off the handle, strong characters such as Ian perhaps more than most. Whenever I realize that Ian doesn't want to talk to me, I know I can rely upon one or two of our friends to say the right things to him and help him to put things into their true perspective. Viv is the foremost of these friends. Not only is he able to help Ian and myself in this way but he has proved a pillar of strength to his godson Liam as well. Liam too suffered a great deal at this time and found Uncle Viv a tremendous support. In the same way that Ian dismisses things while talking to me, I think perhaps that we both did the same with our children, not knowing really what we could safely say. Somehow Viv found the right words and said them when they were needed. Years earlier he had travelled many miles to attend Liam's christening, not wanting to be a proxy godfather. Being Liam's godfather was important to him then and he still takes it very seriously.

Alan and Ian were in constant contact for the next few days, preparing the case for the disciplinary hearing to be held at Lord's. We heard constant rumours of how lenient or severe the penalties were to be. They ranged from a fine to a ban for life from all first-class cricket. It was noticeable that the Ray Illingworths, the Denis Comptons, the Cedric Rhoades's of this world had a field day. Nothing less than hanging, drawing and quartering would suit them!

I travelled to London with Ian the evening before the hearing to attend an Amnesty International gathering. During this evening it was announced that Ian and Viv had challenged each other to a match in aid of Amnesty International. It was a star-studded occasion. Richard Branson made the announcement. In his speech he referred to what was happening in Ian's life at the time, saying that he was sure everyone present, in addition to the general public, were behind Ian and that he hoped the authorities were also. His speech received a tremendous amount of applause with lots of hear, hear's. Feeling much better after this, I was able to enjoy the rest of the evening.

When Ian travelled to hear his fate at Lord's the next day I, as arranged, left to spend the day with Susie Emburey. The time crawled by as I waited for the telephone to ring, advising me of what had happened. Alan

rang, but only to say there was no result yet. I soldiered
on, exchanging small talk with Susie. Finally, Ian rang to
tell me that he had been banned from all first-class cricket
for eight weeks. Quickly, before I could draw breath to
speak, he went on: 'I'm coming over with John [Emburey].
Their game had finished so he's waited for me, I'll be with
you soon.' I was numbed and angry but had half expected
it; there had been so much speculation I knew that
something bad had to happen. It had been a difficult day
for Susie, she knew what it was like for me as John had
previously been banned for three years because he had
played cricket in South Africa. Susie has been a wonderful
friend to me throughout Ian's cricketing career and was
able to find just the right words to say to me at this time.

John had proved invaluable to Ian, slipping him out
through back ways at Lord's to avoid the gaggle of
reporters and television crews. Denis Compton was later
to reprimand him for this kind action quite vehemently. Is
he, I wonder, without imperfection?

Having consumed enough wine, on my part, and
whisky, on Ian's, to calm our nerves we were driven to
join our family at Alan and Ray Dyer's home just outside
London. Ian had suggested before this that, if the hearing
went badly, we should go away together to stay out of the
public eye. I couldn't pre-judge Ian's reaction to whatever
was going to happen, and I felt I would need some moral
support. By this time, having had no let-up from hassle
since February, I was bruised and battered myself and I
knew I couldn't cope with Ian's unpredictable reactions at
this time. Alan is another friend, like Viv, to whom Ian
will listen and who is a strong and calm enough character
to smooth troubled waters, preventing him from taking
too impulsive an action, while Ray is always ready to listen
and help with sound advice. So it was to these two good
friends we turned at this time.

I remember arriving at their home. Liam and Sarah were waiting anxiously for us. Liam ran forward, 'Are you all right, Dad?' he questioned. Sarah flung herself forward and gave Ian a big hug.

We sat and talked and drank while Ian's plans for the future grew wilder and wilder. The three of us just listened, allowing him to say anything he liked, knowing that it was anger and frustration talking and that disagreeing with him now would be totally out of place. Alan had earlier spent some time with Ian on his own, preaching sound sense. Thankfully it was that which Ian later remembered.

I found the press reaction the next day strange, expecting a thorough lambasting. We did, in fact, get support from many quarters. You may have gathered by now that I have little time for reporters in general but there are specific exceptions, exceptions proving the rule. John Woodcock from *The Times*, Matthew Engel of the *Guardian*, Frank Keating and Dudley Doust are among those we have always found to be accurate and fair. I think it is reasonable to blame much of Ian's notoriety on the press in general. They decided that because Ian is aggressive and vital on the field of play he must be portrayed as just that in his private life also. I am in no way trying to say that my husband is whiter than white (tell me one person who is!); what I do say is that certain sections of the press, the gutter press as they have been labelled, blow the tiniest incident out of all proportion, putting ideas into people's minds and twisting and turning events and words until there is absolutely no resemblance to the original action. It is horrific that large sums of money are handed over to anyone who is prepared to put their name to a story which can be greatly distorted or even completely fabricated.

When talking to sports journalists I find much of the blame is attached to the editor of a newspaper who, according to whim, will demand a 'knocking story' or a 'build-up' one. Some editors must, in my opinion, be despicable characters – the way they seem to delight in stories that can only hurt innocent wives, children, parents and families. I often wonder if these people were ever born into a family or if, like Topsy, 'they just growed'. I can't think they would enjoy having their wives or husbands and children subjected to the soul-destroying reports we have had to face. As the children have grown older they have had to share in our troubles. They say little but I know they have suffered deeply and been hurt time and time again by people who, because of what they read, hit out at them, not Ian. You see, it doesn't hurt Ian; he is big and strong both in body and mind and can take it. It is we who hurt. Sarah, at seven, hardly smiled for a whole year following the Lindy Fields affair while Liam became quiet and moody one minute, aggressive the next. Totally out of character for them both. My other point is that 'mud sticks' is a very true saying. All that has gone before is raked up time and time again. Even when a documentary is meant to be a family one, or a purely sporting one, often with glowing, complimentary praise of Ian, inevitably, somewhere, during the programme the old headlines will appear: 'Ian and Kathy Botham arrested on drugs charge'; 'My night of passion with Ian Botham'. Totally irrelevant but always included.

What completely defeats my understanding are those journalists who abuse their privileged position in our lives. Because of our friendship with Brian and Viv Close we had come into contact with several such people. When I was a child, Don Mosey had frequently been included in social occasions at which I was present. When I met and married Ian he contacted us and Ian was invited on several occasions to play in celebrity golf tournaments which he had arranged. We stayed with friends of Don's and all met up for meals. Frankly, they were one of those things Ian could have done without, but because of our family friendship he agreed to take part. I really don't know how, why or when the relationship soured but now Don writes or says nothing remotely complimentary. Recently he has published a book about Ian – a biography. For the background to this he interviewed a great many people but not Ian's mother, father, brother, sisters, wife, in-laws or any other family members. He has included, however, some stories from the past that only someone who has been in a privileged position as a family friend could have known.

There have been several books written about Ian which he has known nothing about. Many people have made a good deal of money out of writing about him without his knowledge or consent, something which I think is wrong. I do believe in freedom of the press, but I also believe in a responsible press. In this matter the law of libel has been proved most unsatisfactory, too long-winded and too costly.

In recent years we have made many friends who have reached the top of their own professions – not only sportsmen but also in the fields of business, politics and law. They have always been anxious to wine and dine with Ian and frequently exhorted him to contact them if ever he needed any help. How significant it was that when we did turn to them help was singularly lacking. Now, however, we are once again being included on the guest lists. I don't propose to mention names but if they read this book I'm sure they will recognize themselves.

Immediately following the ban, we returned home as a family. This was an event to us, as never before during the summer months had we spent more than a day or two all together. Apart from the initial anger I think we adapted very well. I knew I could rely upon Ian's ability to exclude the immediate past and this ability didn't forsake him. He didn't pine for cricket in any way; in fact he hardly mentioned it, although he did watch the Test matches on television. I confess here that I was secretly pleased that they were unable to win without him. I wasn't allowed to say this, though, as he was genuinely hoping for an England win and for good performances from his friends. During the Headingley Test, Ian spent a day there as a guest of the Yorkshire Committee. I believe Brian (Close) with whom he spent a lot of the time received quite a bit of condemnation for inviting him.

The eight-week ban turned out to be a happy time. I knew Ian would find it difficult to spend the whole of it at home. I suppose if you are never able to stay in one place for very long then it is difficult to settle down and do just that. I wasn't really surprised to hear that he wanted to learn to fly a helicopter. I knew that it had been a secret ambition of his for some time so he had my blessing to pack up and go to Shoreham for his lessons. Dedicated and single-minded as ever, he spent three weeks there, returning at weekends to pick up first me, then Liam to show off to us. At the end of three weeks he passed all his exams with flying colours – another record for the books. The one black spot of this period was the now infamous 'gin-slinging dodderers' episode. Ian had been asked to do a question-and-answer evening to raise funds for a family sports centre in Manchester. It was going to be a fun evening, with a few jokes in a relaxed atmosphere. In his introductory speech, Murray Birnie, a long-time friend of Ian's, stated: 'This is going to be a fun evening for everyone. There are no reporters here. Whatever is said is not for publication. Relax and enjoy yourselves.' In one of his replies to a question Ian referred to the selectors as 'gin-slinging dodderers' – a term he has used over the years time and time again. In its rightful context as a joke it is not, and is not intended to be, abusive. A freelance journalist unknown to anyone had taperecorded the whole thing and sold it to a national newspaper for an impressive sum of money. Once again Ian was in the mire. The selectors themselves took it for what it was, a joke, and many who had been selectors over the years laughed with Ian about it. The powers of the TCCB, however, took it more seriously and there were threats of more disciplinary hearings before the whole thing was finally dropped.

I was pleased for the children that Ian was at home now. He was able to take Sarah horse-riding and see for himself how well she was doing. When Liam and Ian had been invited to play in a boys versus parents cricket match, it was great to be able to accept for them both and see them go off together in their whites. Ian was not brought before the disciplinary committee for bringing the game into disrepute following this match, even though when the bowler, Liam, appealed for an lbw the batsman, Ian, strode up the wicket and tweaked his ear! Baby Becky had a new nursemaid – Daddy – who vied with Diane for bathtimes and cuddles, though he did draw the line at nappy-changing. In all it was a happy time. We were even able to turn the tables on one of the reporters. The *Daily Express* rang asking to speak to me.

'Mrs Botham?'

'Yes,' I replied.

'I'm very sorry to have to trouble you at this time.'

'Yes?'

'I understand you and your husband have separated.'

I laughed. 'Where on earth have you got that information from? Just hang on a minute. I'll ask Ian to have a word with you. He's here standing by my side!'

'Oh no, Mrs Botham, there's no need.'

Ian took the phone from me and had more than a few words with him. Unfortunately, Sarah overheard this and, realizing the gist of it, burst into tears. It was then we realized how much recent events had affected her. Ian took her off for a long heart-to-heart talk which did them both good. Being the middle child in our family is a difficult position. Liam is the son and the eldest, he is good at sport and he and Ian have a very special relationship; they go off together as often as possible and he, being a boy, can go with Ian to places where Sarah cannot. Rebecca is the baby who is making up for the fact that Ian saw so little of the others when they were young; she also has a special place in our hearts. Sarah is special too, but finds it difficult to realize this. She wants to do the things that Liam does, she wants the cuddles that Becky gets. We try to give them to her but have to combine them with the discipline that being eight years old demands. We decided then that I should take her on holiday when Ian returned to cricket, just her, leaving Liam and Becky behind. I arranged to go with a friend, Sue Atkinson, and her daughter Kirsten and son Nicholas to Portugal. Sarah was busily planning it, delighted about the whole idea, revelling in the fact that she was doing something the others couldn't.

The eight weeks of Ian's ban flew past. All too soon it was time for Ian to return to first-class cricket. I really didn't expect him to be chosen for the Test matches that summer – too many people had said that he wouldn't be. I was, therefore, quite taken aback when on the Saturday before Sarah and I were to fly off to Portugal, Ian rang to say that he had heard he was included in the team for the final Test at the Oval.

Immediately I knew this, the old pressures returned. I had desperately wanted this holiday to be carefree for Sarah's sake. It is difficult to understand if you are not in my position. I wanted Ian to be back where I knew he wanted to be, but I knew he would have to do well. He had to turn in a good performance now more than ever before, for I fully realized what would be said of him if he didn't. It didn't in the least worry me that I had arranged to be away. I never thought of rearranging my plans, in fact I think it was possibly better that I wasn't around. Jean Rook had interviewed me after the 'Barbados Affair'. We had got on well together and she had, in fact, written a very complimentary article. She now wrote an article advising me to stick with Ian during this time and not go off abroad, more or less saying that there would be others who would be only too willing to take my place by his side. She doesn't know Ian as well as I do and she didn't know the reason behind the holiday either.

The way Ian bounced back into Test cricket is history. The public turned up in their thousands to support him, he took a wicket with his first ball, two more shortly afterwards, first breaking then overtaking Denis Lillee's world record of 355 Test wickets. Later in the match he was well on the way to a fast century when rain stopped play in time to save the New Zealanders from almost certain defeat. It would have been their first defeat in Test cricket that summer – as the newspaper headlines screamed 'Botham is back'. He was a hero once more.

I was sunning myself in Portugal, oblivious to all this. I had travelled, not wanting to know anything about the cricket. Really, I suppose I should say I didn't want to know anything bad. I was definitely not amused therefore when greeted immediately on arrival by a helpful gentleman who first informed me that Ian was in the team, then promised to keep me posted as to what was happening in the match.

Sarah and I had a wonderful holiday together and returned to tell Daddy all about it. We were completely upstaged by the news that Somerset had sacked Viv Richards and Joel Garner. Ian discussed this and all its implications with me, true to his recent promise to start to include me in all aspects of his life. In no way did I want to influence his decision but I was delighted when he decided to leave Somerset in support of his two friends. At the end of the previous season he had been warned by a committee member that he believed there was a move afoot to get rid of Viv, Joel and Ian. Ian had locked this away in part of his brain but I remembered it and when he asked me outright what I thought he should do, I said it was time for a change.

Nineteen eighty-six was the year of enlightenment. First the Barbados affair threw everything into relief. Immediately following that, Ian and I had found a new awareness of each other. The ban had given us our family life and Ian became aware of how much he was missing by leaving us behind so often. The Somerset affair forced him into a change of club which made him think about a complete change all round. Cricket is his life, it is what he does best, so he looked at things on offer other than touring in the winter months. He wanted to spend more time with us all. In accepting a contract with Queensland it meant we could spend weeks out in Australia with him over the next two or three years rather than sit at home while he toured first Pakistan, then India. It was a way of obtaining some stability. No longer are we totally dependent upon the whims of selectors for our winter months. More importantly, I hope it will remove us from the full glare of publicity. During the last tours Ian has been very conscious of the damage this was doing not only to him, but to other members of the team who were constantly under media scrutiny when he was around. He literally had to lock himself away, living in isolation except when I was there, and this was doing no one any good.

This was further highlighted at the end of the Australian tour. We were nearing the end of our stay in Sydney for the final Test when Mark Austin of BBC Sport came up to me and asked if it were not possible for me to stay on until the end of the tour, telling Ian and me that a woman journalist from the *News of the World* had asked him to introduce her to Ian. Other sports journalists were warning us that the 'hatchet' men and women had arrived. My presence was obviously spoiling their stories so, not able to get at Ian, one of them turned his attention to nine-year-old Liam. This journalist's invented story about Liam wasn't in fact printed, but it caused a great deal of heartache to us all, not least to Liam who was devastated by the prospect of being the centre of an untrue media sensation. Elton John, himself the target of press speculation, was wonderful with Liam, taking him under .is wing and sharing with him the jelly and ice-cream prepared for him following his throat operation. What a caring person Elton is, as too is Bob Halle, his PA. We spent a great deal of time with Elton in Australia where he became part of the family. Since we have known him he has been sensitive to our problems and supportive of us all through thick and thin. For Ian a true guide, philosopher and friend.

This last tour of Australia in 1986–87 was a good tour. Ian did well and the team did well, but Ian spent a lot of the time when I wasn't there behind the locked doors of his suite. Much has been made of him having a suite in each hotel the team visited, but I can assure you it was necessary: not only for when we all arrived, but chiefly because in it he could entertain his friends in privacy, free from prying eyes and ever-listening ears. I'm sure the team appreciated it also, because they had many happy hours behind those closed doors celebrating their many and varied wins.

Because of all the furore early in 1986, whether or not I liked it I was pushed into the limelight. Friends and family suggested I should make it work for me. The odd notes I had made of my life over the years were dragged out of a drawer and the passing thoughts I had occasionally entertained of writing a book on my life became a reality. I said 'yes' rather than 'no' more often to requests for appearances and even did one or two modelling and advertising assignments.

When it was suggested that I should walk alongside Ian on another charity walk, this time from Belfast to Dublin, I was ready to say 'yes', and Ian was more than delighted to have me with him. It gave me tremendous satisfaction and a deeper understanding of a lot of things. Why it took so long for Ian to unwind after the last leukaemia walk, for example. The effort, both mental and physical, which goes into a long walk like this was incredible, together with the victory of will-power over pain. Don't ever let me hear anyone say that Ian does it to improve his image. This has been said and it is unfair, unjust and untrue. We gain a great amount of pleasure from these walks, and a unique bond of fellowship is forged between those suffering from this dreadful disease, and those dedicated to defeating it, namely the POWs – Prisoners of the Walk – among whom I am now proud to be numbered. As I walked with Ian, Liam, Sarah and Becky through the centre of Dublin to complete the walk to the Mansion House, I cast a glance to right and left. Barry McGuigan, Alex Higgins, Willie John McBride and Mike Gibson were there then, and I thought of the other famous men and women who had joined him in the thousand and odd miles he has now walked for leukaemia. Not too many people are able to lead a crusade but Ian has managed it, as he manages to do most things he sets out to do.

During a speech at the end of the walk in Dublin Ian complimented me on walking the full 150 miles with him and challenged me to the trek across the Alps in 1988 in aid of the same good cause. Nursing my swollen feet and ankles I accepted the challenge and I shall be there. He also referred to past times of pressure, admitting that as this builds within him he knows how difficult he can be to live with. I took this as a compliment, I know it was intended as one. We are together still, and as I look back over the pages of this book I wonder how or even why. Life has been at times difficult, at times bloody impossible, but these times have been far outnumbered by the good, the funny, the tender and the loving times. As a family we have been welded together, united against adversity – children, grandparents, brother, sisters and all, closely knit. I look forward to the future, always conscious of the fact that to live with a legend can be wonderful but is seldom easy.